CONFESSIONS
OF A BI-POLAR
MARDI GRAS
QUEEN

CONFESSIONS
OF A BI-POLAR
MARDI GRAS
QUEEN

Marie Etienne

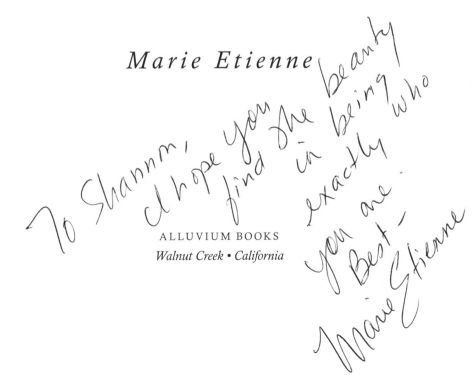

ALLUVIUM BOOKS
Walnut Creek • California

ALLUVIUM BOOKS
3335 Freeman Road
Walnut Creek, CA 94595

Alluvium Books
3335 Freeman Road
Walnut Creek, CA 94595
Tel: 925/947-1282   Fax: 925/274-0733
www.marieetienne.com

FIRST EDITION

For information about special discounts for bulk purchases, please contact Midpoint Trade Books at www.midpointtrade.com or 212/727-0190 or Alluvium Books at mestorge@pacbell.net

Book Design & Layout by
⏛ theBookDesigners

Printed in the United States of America

February 16, 2009

Library of Congress Cataloging-in-Publication Data has been applied for.

ISBN-13: 978-0-9748474-1-2
ISBN-10: 0-9748474-1-0

To my sons

Contents

Acknowledgements

I AM DEEPLY grateful to my editors for their enthusiasm and good counsel. Sam Prestianni, in particular, for his irreverent sense of humor and astute green pen. I've never laughed so hard after hours in a Literature classroom. A very special thanks to Ferrell for her tenacity and keen sense of knowing when to stop. Thank you Marsha Ginsburg and Peggy Vincent for your thoughtful and close readings.

My gratitude to Lynne Meade for her constant support and insight. Each and every Thursday morning, for years, we've walked laps around the Lafayette Reservoir. Thank you for listening to my stories and for helping me find the truth.

I want to thank Judy Folden for her help and support. And special thanks to Kylee for being such a beautiful model. To theBookDesigners (Usana Shadday, Ian Shimkoviak, Alan Hebel and Scott Erwert) for a handsome book.

Most of all, I am grateful to my sons. Your love means the world to me. I'm so proud of you both. I'm a better person for knowing and loving you. I know you still hate the title of this book, so I say: Saaa-weeee.

CONFESSIONS
OF A BI-POLAR
MARDI GRAS
QUEEN

CHASING
YOUR TAIL

A YOUNG RABBIT once said to a wise old rabbit, "Life is so unfair. I've found happiness . . . but it's in my tail. I keep chasing my tail and can't ever catch it. Why is this?"

The wise rabbit smiled. "I, too, have discovered happiness is in my tail. I also found if I just go about my business, it always follows me."

The young rabbit paused then twitched her nose. "Whatever." An instant later, she rushed off to pursue something curious in the distance.

Although the youngster hopped and looped and twirled, the old rabbit did not lose hope. He waited. Being wise, he knew the young rabbit's journey would lead her back to the same question and then to understanding.

DON'T
LOOK AT ME

I N JUNE OF 2005, my sons, Austin and Zack, stayed with their dad for a week while I attended a fiction writing class at University of Iowa. On the fourth day, the instructor asked for a volunteer. The Asian woman seated to my right, the one who almost always mumbled, "Pass," when we were called on to share our previous night's writing, slipped her hands under the desk and lowered her head as if to make herself as inconspicuous as possible. The teacher didn't specify the nature of the exercise, but because I wanted every opportunity for feedback on my manuscript, I raised my hand.

"Marie, sit in the middle of the circle so that everyone can see you."

The Asian woman looked up and grabbed her pen, twisting it in her hands. All twelve faces in the room now turned my way.

Changed my mind, I wanted to say. Pick someone else.

With my heart thumping, I scooted back my chair and

slowly walked to the center of the room. I pulled the hem of my pink and yellow sundress over my knees and crossed my ankles. I regretted not having taken five minutes that morning to shave my legs.

"Look at Marie," the instructor said.

Oh, shit.

"We'll go around the room describing her. We're looking for readily verifiable observations only. No judgments. No assumptions."

He nodded to the journalist who had written her first crime novel.

"She's got blond hair with a slight green tint. Must be a swimmer."

"Blond hair and green tint are valid observations. Whether or not she is a swimmer is an assumption. Keep going." He pointed to the man to her left.

"She's tan."

"Okay. Next."

I turned toward the young woman who'd stopped practicing law to write and care for her four children. Her critiques often sounded like a prosecutor's opening arguments. I forced a smile and held my breath.

"She's wearing diamond earrings and they're real."

"That they're real is an assumption," said the man next to her.

"No," the woman argued. "They're real. Aren't they?"

I looked at the instructor to see if I should respond.

"Fine. They're real. Next."

One by one they went around pointing out my features: hazel eyes, glasses, ankle bracelet, diamond ring on right hand versus the left, yellow floral dress with butterflies, silver watch, blonde hair pulled into a French twist with a white clip, straight white teeth, red lipstick.

"What about her weight?" the instructor said. "Is she old or young? Wrinkled? . . . Don't be so polite."

The teacher nodded to the man seated in front of me. I'd read his manuscript the night before. This nerdy-looking science teacher had bludgeoned to death his protagonist's wife on the first page. I'm doomed. Here comes the hatchet.

"She has large breasts," he said. The class chuckled. I felt my face grow hot. He shrugged. "Sorry."

"No apologies necessary," the teacher said. "Now in your writing, you might consider whether the character displays her endowment proudly or modestly. Does she wear tight, low-cut sweaters or conservative clothing? And word choice. Are they seen as breasts, tits, boobs or bosoms?"

I pulled at the back of my dress to cover more of my chest.

"She's got an athletic build," the Korean woman said. She'd written a hilarious sketch where a mentally handicapped guy tried wooing his teacher by speaking only in Prince lyrics.

The next man added, "But she's a bit overweight for her height."

Here come the spider veins around the nose. The chipped front tooth. Big nose. My hands were trembling. It felt as if the class was gathering momentum to make some cruel, honest observations.

"There are fine wrinkles around her eyes . . . her toe nails are painted red but not her fingernails . . . she wore braces—"

"Assumption!"

And an incorrect one at that.

"She's got a few brown age marks on her cheeks," the young diamond expert said.

Just wait. You'll have them one day.

"Now let's make some assumptions based on what we see."

"Will you turn toward me?" the Asian lady whispered.

I swung my legs around and smiled at her.

After a minute, she said, "She's comfortable with her body and her sexuality."

"Why do you say this?" asked the instructor.

"Because she's willing to sit up here and have twelve people basically undress her with their eyes. She looks so at ease with herself."

I pictured the mallards at Heather Farms gliding across the lake, leaving only the smallest wake while below the surface their little feet paddled frantically to keep them afloat.

The journalist said, "There's a lilt when she speaks. It doesn't sound particularly Southern. More Australian. It's sweet. Child-like. As if she's not quite confident in expressing herself."

"I disagree," the next woman said. "She seems very confident."

"Would the rest of you agree?" the teacher asked.

Some nodded. Some shrugged.

"You're not convinced," he said to a retired business executive who was having his life story ghost-written by the marketing woman seated beside him.

"There's a certain vulnerability in the way she holds herself. I think she tries to appear confident but I don't completely buy it. God bless her willingness to sit here and be scrutinized."

Time to fly out of this pond before I drown.

As if reading my mind, the teacher said, "We're about out of time. Any other comments?"

Another woman said, "You've banned clichés in here . . . but something about her wide eyes says deer caught in the headlights. I see, not terror exactly, but something in her face. Despite the smile."

My hands froze in my lap. My neck tensed.

"Thanks, Marie. This leads us to our next exercise . . ."

I returned to my desk wondering how much they would have uncovered if given more time. Did they really not see all the other imperfections I saw in the mirror? Maybe because we're all strangers, and of no real consequence in each other's lives after this week—unlike, at times, family and friends—there was no reason to harshly judge or point out more brutal flaws. As the teacher explained the next assignment, I thought about how I had automatically assumed (i.e., feared) the worst feedback.

A few years earlier I'd been at a spa with three girlfriends, all of us in our late thirties. Two of the women were in the kitchen area of the suite looking for a wine opener. Just as I bit into a second chocolate truffle, the fourth women—beautiful, long-legged—pulled me aside. She said, "I've got something to tell you."

I'd first met her back when I was six months pregnant with Zack. Even before we shook hands, she said, "Jeepers. You're so huge." Now I feared she'd tell me I was disgusting and should think about doing a few hundred sit ups instead of cramming my face with candy. I dropped the uneaten portion of the truffle back into the box.

She glanced back at two women and then whispered,

"I met this guy online. He's coming here this weekend. He doesn't know I'm married."

Oh, my God. She's flirting with some guy in cyberspace and about to embark on a stupid affair that could ruin her marriage. What a relief.

"It just seemed like harmless fun," she said. "But now—"

"Don't do it," I said. "Even if the guy has a King Kong pecker."

"You're right." She lifted the tied ends of her sarong and pulled at the fringe. "I'm so embarrassed," she said and looked down at the carpet.

"You haven't done anything yet that can't be fixed. Besides, you want to hear something really warped?"

She nodded.

"I thought you were going to fuss at me about eating these chocolates. Tell me that I was a pig."

"Really?"

I shrugged. "Guess my mind has been conditioned to think that way. You're so good about your diet, and here I am, the overweight one, eating like—"

"Stop," she said and placed her hand on my arm. "Enough already."

Okay, so maybe I was a little self-absorbed. But then I'd been trained by the best.

• • •

T HE AUGUST BEFORE I started fourth grade, my father convinced my mother that corralling the eight youngest children into two Cadillacs and driving in the middle of hurricane season to several destinations—Galveston, Grand Canyon, Six Flags, Carlsbad Caverns—was a sane idea of a vacation.

"Just imagine, Bump," my father said, using the nickname they shared as a private joke. "No cooking. No cleaning. Check into a Holiday Inn in Houston on Sunday and by Tuesday you're at the Holiday Inn in El Paso."

If I were my mother, I would have probably wanted to whack him on the head and respond, "Hey, Doofus. Why do you think we built this brick house with nineteen rooms? It wasn't so I could be with the children."

Daddy failed to consider that confining a brood of eight bickering kids to two cars for six hours a day might make you want to swerve into the next eighteen-wheeler that passed by. Momma relented but not happily.

As the trip progressed, Daddy's mood more closely resembled Momma's.

At one Howard Johnson's roadside cafe, the younger kids pushed and shoved and argued over the seating arrangement until he gave us *the look*. I grabbed the empty chair next to him and ordered fries and a BLT *without* mayonnaise.

My aversion to mayonnaise came from a disgusting tale my teenage brother Chess had told my sisters and me when I was four. In the story, a creepy man, supposedly living in the swamps in Louisiana, squeezed out his zits on his bumpy face to make a special mayonnaise that he sold in town. Although four summers had passed since we sat in the dressing room above our swimming pool and listened to my brother tell this story, I thought of pus every time I looked at a jar of Hellmann's.

An old couple was seated in the next booth. The man said, "Nice looking bunch of kids you got there." I waited for Daddy's usual response about having his own little harem but he simply nodded.

Soon our lunch was delivered. I bit into my BLT and tasted the mayonnaise. I spat the soggy bite into my napkin and when my father wasn't looking tossed the bundle under the table. Now Daddy would have a fit if I asked the waitress for another sandwich. He never complained in restaurants. It seemed stupid to me to pay a lot of money for something you couldn't eat. But that was how he was.

I figured a way to get rid of the mayonnaise. Using a tooth-pick, I wiped off the white dressing from each little triangle of toasted bread. My younger brothers and sisters ate quickly. They wanted to look around the gift shop before Daddy paid the bill.

"Momma, can I go to the bathroom?" my younger sister Anne asked as Daddy removed a bill from a wad of hundreds in his wallet. He had taken only a couple bites of his hamburger but I didn't blame him. Rubbery ground beef was gross, too.

Before the waitress returned with his change, Daddy was standing and buttoning his jacket. Even on vacation he wore his work suits.

"Dibs on Daddy's car," I yelled, squinting into the bright sunlight. Four of us piled into the Eldorado and the others went with Momma.

Once we'd all settled into our seats, Daddy pushed in his cigarette lighter then jerked around. "That was the most disgusting display of manners I have ever witnessed," he yelled.

There was no pretending he wasn't talking to me. His dark eyes pinned me to the upholstery, and even if I had wanted to, I couldn't have moved. He grabbed my teenage brother Chess's headrest so hard his knuckles turned white. Claire and Amy, my sisters, seated on opposite sides of me, stiffened and pulled away. I swallowed, trying to figure out what I'd done or said.

"You made me sick to my stomach. That was so nasty what you did with the toothpicks. I couldn't eat a thing after you began to mess with your food." He went on about how the couple next to us probably thought he hadn't taught his children any manners. He was humiliated.

I felt my chin wobble. Tears would only make him angrier. "I'm sorry," I mumbled. "I didn't mean to but . . ."

"No buts about it. You *ruined* my appetite. Don't you ever do that again. Do you hear me? Do you?"

"Yes, sir." I nodded. Tears streamed down my checks.

The car lighter clicked. He ignored it and stared at me as if I was some roadside collision that had left him horribly transfixed. Finally, he turned away before every last bit of oxygen had left my body, and with one quick tug, he loosened his tie. Before he started the car, he tapped a fresh Winston against the steering wheel. Tap. Tap. Tap. Soon suffocating smoke filled the car.

For forty-five minutes after Daddy pulled out of the parking the only sound was the radio playing his old-folks big-band music and the clicking of the turn signal when he got behind someone who drove even slower than he did.

Chess glanced back at Momma's car, which trailed the

bumper of Daddy's Eldorado. "I don't see Anne," he said to Daddy.

"Oh, hell," Daddy said and looked in the rearview mirror. We all peered out the back window. He struck the turn signal. Of course it was my fault because if I hadn't grossed out my father, he wouldn't have been in such a rush to get to the car and scream at me, and he would have noticed my sister had never come out of the bathroom. He pulled off to the side of the highway. Momma stopped behind him.

Daddy got out of the car and slammed the door.

"Better hope she's in there," Chess said.

"Shut up. It's not my fault."

"What difference does that make?"

My father returned to the car without saying a word. He took the next exit and soon we were headed back the way we'd come. We drove to the restaurant in silence.

Luckily, my little sister was okay. The waitress sat her at the counter with paper and crayons, figuring eventually we'd notice we were short one kid. Daddy came out of the restaurant with Annie in his arms. He must have been so relieved to find her unharmed; he didn't bother to yell at me again.

As a parent, I've occasionally revisited that afternoon, and it occurs to me how differently my sons would have handled such a rebuff.

"But that's not fair, Mom," Austin, now fifteen, would say. "How come you acted so normal in the restaurant and now you're being so mean?" Thirteen-year-old Zack would say, "We didn't do it on purpose to embarrass you."

Perhaps a girl with a little more insight and courage might have said to her father, "If you were so bothered by my table manners, why wait until we got to the car? And besides, why would you worry about how *you* looked if I'm the one with the bad manners?" Perhaps she wouldn't see herself for decades as far less than perfect. Someone who makes others recoil. Someone unlovable who shouldn't be inspected up close.

Until this incident, my father had seemed the more loving, safer parent. At times he lost his temper. But Momma, she was the mean one. She was the parent who would look up from the stove and shriek to see that overnight my eye had swollen shut with greenish pus and dried blood. Unconcerned with my vision, she only feared what her friends might think. She was the one who would ask, "What in the hell have you done?" As if I'd planned the whole eye infection—including the subsequent shots into my eyelids and searing hot compresses—just to taunt her and her fragile self-esteem.

Soon, the *Howard Johnson's Incident* was followed by the *String Bean Incident.* If you're going to eat beans with your fingers, don't do it in the presence of your father when he's in the middle of an important phone call. Then there was the *Blue Eye Shadow Faux Pas* that ruined my eighth grade school photo. Luckily, I never had much of an acne problem, like some of my siblings, so I was spared Daddy's ridicule and rejection when he was forced to leave the dinner table because someone's complexion had turned his stomach inside out.

Over time, I learned that survival meant being invisible. It was okay to stand out from my eight siblings when it came to work, school, and artistic achievements, but from a physical standpoint, I simply wanted to be unseen. For so much of my early life, my parents' attention seemed steeped in disgust and disapproval.

I often tell my sons to be careful what they say to someone they love. If one hears something enough times—you're ugly, you're stupid, not good enough, unlovable—soon she will believe it.

THROW ME SOMETHING
MISTER

A T FOURTEEN, I phoned my boyfriend and told him the bad news: "I'm breaking up. You're not enough of a challenge."

I stood on the patio in my navy blue polka-dot bikini, a puddle of water collecting on the pebbled concrete, and waited for his response. Our black Labrador puppy barked at the splashing, squealing, and laughter in the backyard. My sisters and friends were squeezing every last bit of fun out of this final week of summer vacation by diving off the board, slipping down the water slide, and springing off the trampoline into our swimming pool. I was, too, before deciding to dump a nice guy.

"You want a challenge?" he finally said, disbelief and hurt commingled in his thick Cajun accent.

For me there was greater value in scarcity than abundance, in things just beyond my reach. I was used to standing on the curb among masses of Mardi Gras party-goers, waving my arms as the masked float riders inched their way past me. I'd spent my childhood jumping up and down, yelling, "Throw me somethin', mister," doing anything short of flashing my breasts to stand out from the crowd. And whenever I realized I'd caught the masked man's eyes, I'd hold my breath in antici- pation. Would he choose me? Yet within seconds of having a handful of doubloons or other precious trinkets tossed my way, the thrill of the quest died. If the baubles made it home, I'd stuff them in drawers or in the garbage. It was no different with hard-won love and affection.

When I didn't answer his question, he said, "Would it help to know I made out with a girl at a party last night?"

I smiled. "Was she cute?"

"Kind of."

He didn't sound convincing. "This isn't going to work anymore," I said.

His affection had come to feel like the August humidity— cloying and damp. Sure, he was sweet, goofy sweet. But way too easy. And way too nice. There must have been something wrong with him. He must have had some defect that other girls perceived and passed on. Besides, I wanted a challenge, something valuable, elusive, something that couldn't be had so easily. I wanted to stand on the curb, giddy with anticipa- tion, and feel the excitement of the catch.

I suspect this attraction to emotionally unavailable guys started with my father. I adored him. Daddy was John Wayne without the swagger, Lorne Greene without the Ponderosa, Clark Gable without Carole Lombard. Daddy was handsome, eccentric, popular, wealthy, smart, funny, strong, creative, magical, and mysterious. He was also moody, sometimes vio- lent and unstable, often remote. In short, he was an alcoholic and chemically imbalanced.

But the negative qualities were just static on my adoration radar. Whenever I received his attention, love, or approval, it radiated every cell of my being. Like a dope fiend, I craved more.

But fathers sometimes belly-flop off the pedestals they find themselves on when life blows in from all directions. Whenever mine did, I set him up there again. Even when he disappointed me, I'd pretend that he hadn't, and if pretending didn't work, I'd forgive him. Long before his death in 1993, I was on the hunt to find another man to love as much, and I would win his approval.

•••

ONE OF MY COLLEGE BOYFRIENDS, I'll call him "Jimmy," was a perfect example of my imperfect man. Equal parts Cajun and Italian, Jimmy wasn't the tallest guy at a party, he wasn't the handsomest, the cleverest, the most well-mannered or successful, but bar none he was the sexiest twenty-eight-year-old I'd ever met, unruly black hair and all. He could turn a lopsided smile into a promise of Mischief. He found a way to package a huge nose and a goofy just-about-to-sneeze frown with a naughty squint of his green and golden eyes to make your throat dry up.

I'd see him at parties and we'd exchange polite hellos. Like Daddy, Jimmy was constantly surrounded by a loyal clan—drinking buddies, hunting buddies, golfing buddies, boating buddies, poker buddies. His hands were constantly flying in animated gesture. He greeted his pals with a friendly squeeze or slap. His social dexterity was something I envied. My own popularity came with great effort, often leaving me exhausted.

Not only did men seek Jimmy's attention, women did as well. Attractive women in their twenties and thirties buzzed about him like bees to honeysuckle. I'd watch him flirt and tease and I'd tell myself to forget about it.

In the end, it was probably my nonchalance that piqued Jimmy's interest. Or lust. The day after an impromptu poker game where I treated him with no more regard than I did the other guys, he telephoned and invited me to New Orleans for a weekend.

"There's a Saints game and a party," he said. "My cousin offered us his apartment in the Quarter."

What audacity. We hadn't even shared a meal outside the company of friends and here he was suggesting three nights alone in the Big Easy. What kind of girl did he think I was?

"I'll have to check with my boss about taking Monday off," I said, trying to maintain my glee. When we hung up, I danced around my kitchen and hugged myself. Jimmy had chosen me!

No one was home when we arrived at the apartment in the French Quarter. The key wasn't under the doormat or in any of the planters.

"Plan B, Ma-ree," he said and grabbed my suitcase.

"You're such a poet," I said and prayed Plan B didn't involve scratching the game and the party and going back to Lafayette.

We returned to the alley where he'd parked his Volvo, a surprisingly practical car for an often reckless man. He got back on I-10, exiting on Causeway Boulevard toward Metairie. The Landmark Hotel, a funky building with a tall round tower, had always stood as a signpost whenever I'd visited Lafayette's older, more risqué, sister city. Obviously, Jimmy hadn't worked a three-night hotel stay into his budget.

I'd never stayed in a hotel with a man I wasn't actually dating, so it was awkward to find ourselves staring at a king-size bed when we set down our luggage. It didn't help my nervousness that I'd deliberated all week about how long to wait before having sex with Jimmy. Now the question seemed moot. How could we not in such close proximity?

"So this is my room, and yours is where?" I teased.

He threw his bag on the bed and ignored my question.

It turned out that, despite his reputation among many of his pals, Jimmy was a gentleman. After insisting on paying for dinner and all our drinks, he didn't insist on sex that night in bed. Not like my last boyfriend with whom I'd spent an evening in New Orleans and found myself flinching in pain the next morning because he'd fucked me non-stop.

Jimmy and I climbed into bed, me in a sheer nightgown and matching robe my grandmother had given me for my 20th birthday, and him in white briefs. We began kissing. Sloppy, uninhibited, playful kisses. As the make-out session got more urgent, he began pressing himself against me. I pulled away and whispered, "Do you mind if we wait? We don't really know each other yet."

He smiled and traced my lips with his finger before kissing me good-night. By the next afternoon, before we dressed for the party, I'd decided I now knew him well enough.

We had one big upset that weekend. Late Sunday evening, I had to spend forty-five minutes stranded with a couple of his drunk buddies on a corner of Royal Street, holding a souvenir flag and a stale beer while he flirted with some woman across the street. I could understand ignoring each other at gatherings in New Iberia, but now, here together in New Orleans, my feelings were hurt. I wanted to shout, "You don't sleep with a girl and then line up the next one right in front of her!"

On the way back to the hotel, I lowered the car window and turned away from Jimmy. Lighting one cigarette off another, I ignored him when he said, "Are you okay?" The longer his question hung between us unanswered, the faster he drove down Canal. Mardi Gras beads, tossed many months ago and now broken and faded, hung from trees lining the street. Drunk and reckless behind the wheel, Jimmy smeared the city lights into a blur before my eyes.

He made no overtures for sex that night. I lay in bed, staring at the walls, choking on disappointment while he snored.

In the morning, he woke me with a kiss. I felt his stubble brush against my cheek and opened my eyes to see his staring back at me, so green and clear. He frowned like a small boy who'd just been reprimanded. I giggled. He scooted his body an inch closer, and then another inch. Perhaps it was easier to make amends than face two hours of uncomfortable silence in the car. Or had he been so loaded he only vaguely remembered what happened? Maybe he was genuinely remorseful and yet didn't know the right words? Whatever thoughts were behind that frown, I didn't care. I was smitten. I'd caught the Jimmy bug.

After New Orleans, we were a couple for a while. He was my date for a Mardi Gras ball. I was his date at parties. It wasn't long before I fell in love with him, although I never professed it. He played it cool so I did the same. Jimmy was eight years older than me, established in his medical profession, entrepreneurial, financially stable. I loved that he owned a small blue cottage in New Iberia, a perfect little starter home for us and the children.

Though fairly conservative in his dress, he sometimes wore the most unflattering outfits. Picture "Do Ya Think I'm Sexy?" Rod Stewart in too-tight white pants. Rather than take offense at the good-natured teasing these outfits caused, he'd wiggle his cute butt, feeding friends goofy smiles and comebacks that made them want to keep upping the ante. He was a clown with a sober, intelligent side. A buddy of his dated my best friend. This woman and I could be quite catty. When Jimmy heard us ridicule someone, even if it was one of his ex-girlfriends, he wouldn't join in. Often I heard him come to the defense of a guy being unfairly thrashed behind his back. In this way, Jimmy was different from my father. Both my parents could be extremely cruel and they fed on gossip.

Most of all, I loved lying in bed with Jimmy, feeling his hands explore my body, being devoured by his kisses.

But with Jimmy and me, it was always one step forward and three back. Every time we started to get serious, he'd pull his Lone Ranger routine. He'd disappear without a word. No call. No explanation. A week would pass. Then two. Soon a month. And I'd be left wondering, Who was that masked man? What have I done wrong now?

There is a term for men like Jimmy, my father, and others like them. It's a term I didn't know back then, not on an intellectual level. He was not non-committal, scared, or a victim of Peter Pan Syndrome, but he was what we now call emotionally unavailable. My father wouldn't commit to being there when we needed him. Jimmy wouldn't commit either.

In a warped way, he was what I'd asked for: someone who would not love me intimately. The result? He helped preserve my belief that I was unlovable.

Since Jimmy lived in New Iberia and I in Lafayette, a distance of twenty miles (but as effective as two states when you're avoiding someone), it was easy not to bump into each other. I'd hear of Jimmy-sightings from my girlfriends. When the reports changed from "He was alone and looked miserable" (the miserable part for my benefit) to "I think he had a date," I finally told myself we were done. In the early 80's, I believed what I'd been taught: girls didn't chase boys.

Every time I convinced myself I was better off without him, he'd call and say, "Ma-ree! What's going on girl? Let's have dinner." Like a love-sick puppy, one you've ignored for days and left curled up at the door, I'd be there wagging my tail when Jimmy came back. And for a while we couldn't keep our paws off each other. Then his buddies would start complaining, "Can't Jimmy come out to play?" Or another pretty girl would capture his green eyes. Or maybe, despite wanting it to be different, he'd realize once again that I wasn't the right girl for him. The cycle would repeat: a week, a month . . . no calls. Tears. Slammed doors. And eventually, new interests.

In one go-round, when I felt him pulling away, I found myself crying hysterically for days. It was the first time I'd felt the physical pain of needing the love of a man, other than my father. I decided to make a pre-emptive strike. I left a letter at Jimmy's door telling him how I was falling in love with him and rather than wait for his calls to stop completely, I was breaking up now. That got an immediate response.

Seated in an Italian restaurant the next evening, his hands locked with mine at the table, he said he too was falling in love. However, *if* we were to marry, I'd have to stop spending as much time with a certain girlfriend, a mutual friend he claimed partied and gossiped too much. I sat there dumbstruck—he'd said *marry!* I nodded and waited for a more romantic proposal. A little velvet box, perhaps. None.

The next day, the next week, the next month . . . no word from Jimmy. He'd apparently stepped out onto the ledge, looked at the horizon, then glanced down, grabbed his balls, and ran back to the safety of his buddies.

No matter how hard you try, sometimes you can't help who you fall in love with. Sometimes, that love survives, even twenty years later.

• • •

I N THE SUMMER OF 2002, I was on Main Street in New Iberia setting up a reading for the upcoming publication of *Storkbites*, my first memoir, when I ran into an old friend. By this time, I was the divorced mother of two boys, ages nine and seven. We had barely finished hugging hello when she whipped back her long hair and exclaimed, "Jimmy's divorced. He just turned fifty, he's looking good, and wants to have a baby. Call him before some other gal nabs him." Just hearing Jimmy's name made my skin tingle. I'd flown home for various holidays, funerals, and weddings over the years, and always hoped I'd run into him. But I never did. There was no use trying to convince her or me of the geographical futility of such an endeavor. I lived in California. Jimmy, Louisiana. Within minutes she had his secretary on her cell phone.

The next evening, I paced my sister's bedroom, consulting my sixteen-year-old nephew on fashion; his retail job at the mall qualified him, in my eyes, as an expert. My sister looked on, her nose wrinkled. She didn't approve of Jimmy. According to her, once a playboy, always a playboy. She said I was setting myself up to be hurt again. Besides, I was a mother. I should be reading *Harry Potter* to my boys instead of gallivanting off with an old flame.

"Does this sundress scream forty-year-old trying to look like a twenty-year-old?" I pressed the floral fabric against my stomach. My nephew snickered. My sister rolled her eyes. "No time for a tummy tuck?" I said. "Hair . . . up or down? Where did these flabby arms come from? Would a turtleneck be too weird in mid-August?"

The doorbell rang and I startled.

"You look fine, Aunt Marie," my nephew said. He handed me the red sandals we'd decided on, so Dorothy-like in my adventure down the yellow brick road.

My heart raced. Jimmy's back was turned as I entered the den, giving me the luxury of sizing him up first. No shiny, sun-freckled scalp or frightening Donald Trump comb-over. A full head of curly hair that appeared to be leisurely graying. No severe bulge hanging over his slacks. And that great butt. So far, nothing about his appearance disappointed. I called his name and he whirled around.

"Hey thar, Ma-ree." He hugged me tight. His cologne reminded me how his scent would cling to my sheets for days.

We pulled apart and allowed each other a moment to assess the changes, the wear and tear of two decades. I was pleased to see the years of drinking, smoking, and sun had been forgiving. And he still had that goofy, seductive smile.

"Look at you, Miss California gal."

Sun and age had given my brownish hair gold and gray

highlights. He was probably reaching for it when he grazed my bare shoulder. His touch sparked goose bumps. I felt light-headed. It had been five years since my divorce and this was my first real date.

"Where are those boys of yours?" he asked.

We stepped over their scattered toys as he followed me to the loft. The cartoons on the television muted the gurgling sounds of the aquarium pump in the narrow sun-lit room. Daddy's prized marlin, which my sister nabbed after his death, hung on the far wall.

"Austin, Zack, this is Jimmy."

Two milky white heads turned away from the television and faced us. Jimmy extended his hand to Austin. I could tell by my son's flaccid arm that he had no interest in meeting this man. He glanced at Jimmy, then me, then back to the TV screen.

Zack's handshake was a little more enthusiastic. His pupils were fully dilated, as they often were when he was nervous or excited. I imagined the thoughts running through his mind: He doesn't look like Dad; he's old; why does he talk weird?; he seems nice; Mom's acting all funny; she's even got that black stuff on her eyelashes; I wonder if Austin likes him.

"When will you be back?" Austin asked. I sensed he was feeling insecure.

"Not too late, but don't wait up." I'd already told myself I wasn't sleeping with Jimmy. Just two old friends having dinner. But I didn't want to feel rushed either. Who knew if it would be another twenty years or ever if I saw him again? I bent over the futon and kissed each of my boys good-night.

There was a distinct odor of cigars as I climbed into Jimmy's Suburban and watched him walk around the front of the car. How unbelievably lucky that after so many years we were both unattached at the same time, especially considering that between us three marriages and countless relationships had started and ended. As he opened his door, I thought about our first date. He'd walked right into my townhouse, past the suitcase I'd packed for New Orleans, and kissed me, saying, "Just wanted to get that out of the way."

Turning toward him now as he started the car, I said, "You look great."

"Likewise." He squeezed my hand.

I smiled, somewhat disappointed that he didn't lean over and plant a big kiss. We were grownup now. Just two old friends having dinner.

At the restaurant we traded divorce stories. Conversation was easy, familiar. I told him my boys had adjusted to two households. I had the best of both worlds: mom during the week; single and free on weekends to pursue my sports, writing, and hobbies. His first marriage, an oops, ended quickly. His second wife, a widow, had sons whom he helped raise, an opportunity to play dad that he was grateful for. He also wanted to have his own children, at least one, boy or girl, but his wife wasn't interested in starting over. So at the ten-year-mark in his marriage, he left, figuring at fifty it was a long shot—trying to find a suitable partner with whom to have a baby—but it was now or never.

The sparkle in his eyes had faded. His once-animated hands were quieter. He held up his empty wine glass for a refill. Then he said, "So if the stars, moon, and sun ever align, it might just happen."

There was one trait about Jimmy I had completely forgotten. He was frugal. He didn't waste entertainment dollars on appetizers or dessert. I remembered how little we ate that first weekend in New Orleans, how I'd been too shy to suggest we stop drinking for a while to have dinner, how the first thing I did when he dropped me back at my townhouse was order a pizza supreme. I laughed now as he told me how his stepsons drove him crazy by dialing 411. He'd find the charges on his monthly phone bill and storm through the house: "How much effort does it take to open a phonebook!" He scratched the back of his neck when I admitted I was prone to using directory assistance and even the direct dial option at an extra charge.

After dinner we went to a neighborhood club. As soon as we walked into the smoky place, a group of middle-aged men seated at the bar turned and smiled. Jimmy's own grin grew bigger and his swagger more pronounced as we approached the chorus of "Hey, Jimmy boy. What's happening, you scoundrel? What are you doing with such a sweet-looking lady?" He loved being the center of attention.

"This here's Ma-ree Etienne." I loved how he called me Ma-ree. As soon as he said Etienne, a fairly well-known name in town, the guys started asking for my help in figuring out which of my sisters they'd either dated or gone to high school with or knew from Red's Health Club. I was grateful when Jimmy put his hand on my hip and led me away to a booth.

"Would this be your little home away from home?" I said. Jimmy grinned and looked at his buddies who kept glancing in our direction. "Will there be an inquisition tomorrow? Please do be discreet."

"Darling, I'm always discreet." He pulled another cigar from his shirt pocket. He'd become a chain smoker. I tried to imagine being around that toxicity for extended periods of time, and, of course, the boys. But then, this was only a one-night deal.

We talked about my upcoming memoir and the dissent it had caused among my six sisters. "Well, Ma-ree," he said, picking up his cognac, "sometimes it's best to let a sleeping dog lie." He didn't have the easiest upbringing either. I'd heard stories second-hand.

"Do you remember once we went out for margaritas after a football game?" I said. "It was a year before my little brother Nickey committed suicide. Right before I moved to California."

He lit his cigar, took a couple of puffs, then shook his head. His fingers carefully loosened the gold and red band on the brown wrapper.

"Eighteen years old and this was his third stay in rehab. My family and I had just wasted an entire week in group therapy and more of my father's money on trying to help Nickey with his addictions. Instead of revealing anything truthful, we just hinted at stuff, skirted the abuse, the drinking, the neglect, all to protect my parents, to maintain the status quo."

"That was a long time ago, Ma-ree," Jimmy said and leaned in closer. I knew that if he'd scripted the evening, I was certainly deviating from the plan with this topic. But I didn't care. I suddenly wanted more than anything to share something truthful with him, see his reaction.

"We were on our second pitcher of drinks and I started telling you about my childhood. Until then, I'd never told any of my friends about what my parents were really like. I was ashamed, thought they'd think there was something wrong with me. But for some reason, I took a risk with you. For about two hours I went on and on, telling you everything. I remembered you had recently quit smoking and I felt guilty because as you listened to my story you kept reaching for my cigarettes."

I swallowed and sipped my Diet Coke. Jimmy sucked hard on his cigar. I traced the pronounced veins in the hand he pressed on the seat and smiled. I loved his hands.

"Anyway, you were very sweet. You slept over. Held me all night. I felt like, wow, I've just told this guy my deepest, darkest secrets and he doesn't suddenly need to go home to walk the dog."

I nudged his shoulder and he nearly dropped his cigar.

"What's that for?" he asked and brushed ashes off his slacks.

"For vanishing off the face of the Earth. You walked the dog, after all. No bothering with 'Have a nice life, see you around' or anything. You pulled your disappearing act and I was left thinking, 'Shit, Marie. You shouldn't have told all your ugly secrets.'"

He removed a loose piece of tobacco from his tongue, wiped it on the napkin, looked at his buddies at the bar. Was he signaling them: Please rescue me?

"I'm sorry about that," he said, meeting my eyes. "Maybe it hit a little too close to home. Maybe I couldn't deal with it. But that was shitty of me not to call."

I nodded and blinked. I'd waited years, hoping I'd have the courage to tell him that story and hear him apologize.

"Thank you," I said.

After another cognac we left the bar. There was comfortable silence between us as we drove down Pinhook. The road glistened from the rain. I watched the wipers swish back and forth, and I thought of my flight home in less than twelve hours. It occurred to me this might be my last drive through Lafayette with Jimmy. Most likely the stars, moon, and sun would align for him and someone else. He turned into a parking lot of a large office complex.

I looked at him. "Can we get to my sister's house from here?" I said.

He scratched his neck, and said, "Uh, thought I'd show you my new house. But of course if you'd rather, I'll take you home."

I stared at him in disbelief. *You just never change. Buy the girl some dinner. Listen to how you were a bad boy years ago. Then take her home to fuck. She's already said it's been years since her divorce. The old girl probably wouldn't mind doing a little Hokey Pokey with ol' Jimmy boy.*

"No," I said, "I'd like to see your house." I wasn't going to sleep with him. *I wasn't.*

The silence turned awkward. We entered a new tract development of modest homes. The landscaping was still in the infancy stage. The flowering shrubs and trees looked sparse against the brick facades. The arrangements varied slightly from building to the next, but the gardener hadn't stretched his imagination.

In the garage, a yellow tennis ball tethered to the ceiling indicated to Jimmy when he'd reached the wall. I imagined him coming home lit up from a night out with his buddies and all that stood between the hood of his car and the kitchen sink was a fuzzy yellow ball. My boys had never seen me intoxicated. I imagined them asking, "Mom, why's Jimmy's car parked in the kitchen? Why's he acting so funny tonight?"

The narrow foyer led to an open kitchen/family room. He was neat for a bachelor. Much neater than my boys and I were. There were no dirty dishes stacked in the sink. The trash compactor wasn't overflowing with pizza boxes. Six months worth of magazines weren't piled on the tile counters. I smiled when

I noticed the ceiling fan had been sponge-painted to blend into its beige surroundings.

Near the fireplace was a large dog's pillow. The fur on it was blonde, not black like the Labrador he'd had when we'd dated.

"Hunting dog?" I asked, looking for a door leading to the backyard. He nodded.

"Come meet Zeus."

As soon as we neared the door the dog began barking. "Be prepared. He's gonna be wet and wild." I liked puppies. But a hyper full-grown dog, especially when wet, really should be viewed from afar.

Jimmy gave Zeus an opening just wide enough to squeeze his way into the room. I stood behind the ottoman. As he bounded over, I said, "Oh, he's really pretty. Really wet, too. No, no . . . Zeus, don't lick."

"Sit, you stupid boy," Jimmy commanded. The dog ignored him and started sniffing around my crotch like I was his new best friend.

"Go away, now," I said and pushed his nose away from my dress. I looked at Jimmy. "I'm not really much of a dog person."

He laughed and dragged Zeus back outside. After slamming the door, he said, "Well, I'll wash my hands and then show you the rest." The rest included, no doubt, the bedrooms. Remember, Marie: you are not sleeping with this man.

We entered the master bedroom. I stood a safe distance from the mattress and crossed my arms. "Very nice. So your bathroom . . . must be in here . . ."

The tour ended with his home office. He grabbed a pad and pen from the tidy desk and asked for my e-mail address.

I blurted it out so quickly he shook his head, and said, "Once again, Ma-ree."

When we were both seated in his car, waiting for the garage door to open, I said, "Do you remember your black Lab? I think her name was Cosmo."

"Cosmo. That's right." He put the key in the ignition but didn't start the engine.

"Remember how when she was a puppy, the minute we started making love, she'd hear the bed squeaking, and run into the room. She'd stand at the foot of the bed, clawing at the mattress, yelping for us to let her up."

Jimmy stared at me as if he hadn't a clue what I was talking about. How conceited of me. With all the women he's taken to bed, he probably didn't remember a couple of rainy summer afternoons twenty plus years ago. A huge smile formed on his face and his green eyes, no longer dull, twinkled.

"We never seemed to have any problems in that department, did we?"

I blushed. Good save, Jimmy boy.

"She lived to twelve," he said. "She was a good dog."

I listened to a funny story about Cosmo's first hunting trip as we drove to my sister's. When her white fence came into view, I knew the evening was over.

Jimmy got out and walked me to the back door. "I really enjoyed seeing you," I said. He put his hands on my hips and held my stare. Then, thank God, he kissed me. Gently, as if testing my resistance. We pulled apart. Then I kissed him. He pulled me closer. I held on tight. His kiss, like his laugh, had left its imprint on me. My body would know it anywhere.

Part of me wanted to suggest that we skedaddle back to his place. The other part was content just kissing him. The evening ended with promises to e-mail. I wanted to wake up my sister to tell her the news: despite my best efforts, I was, once again, in love with Jimmy. She would have argued it was only lust. And perhaps I'd concede to a large degree that it was. But he'd awakened something inside me, a physical and emotional yearning I'd long feared dead.

I opened the bedroom door quickly so the hall light wouldn't wake the boys. Austin was snoring on the top bunk. Zack lay sprawled on the futon near the closet. After stepping around overflowing suitcases and toys, I climbed onto the lower mattress and waited for my eyes to adjust to the darkness. Until the morning sun nudged my boys from their dreams, I intended to lie there, to replay every word, every kiss Jimmy and I had shared, and to imagine what it'd be like to make love to him after so many years.

Jimmy called the next morning to wish us a good flight home. He followed up with an e-mail: "I had a wonderful evening, Ma-ree. Just for the record, I've always enjoyed spending time with you." For a year, we flirted by e-mail and then the next summer my boys and I again visited Louisiana. This time, I'd given myself permission to do the Hokey Pokey with Jimmy. I figured that if I had to wait another year, I'd go mad.

• • •

TWO MONTHS AFTER OUR SECOND DATE, I scheduled a reading in New Orleans for *Storkbites* and asked Jimmy to join me for the weekend. He agreed.

On a warm September afternoon, exhausted from having spent the previous hours visiting all the independent bookstores in the city, we fell in unison on the hotel bed. A chill traveled through my body. The air conditioning apparently had two settings—blizzard and July.

Jimmy looked at the goose bumps covering my tanned arms. He smoothed the raised blond hair and kneaded my muscles as if I were Silly Putty. Warmth from his body transferred to my mine. I closed my eyes and relaxed. His hands moved up my arm to my shoulder and then to my neck. Below our balcony, Bourbon Street was revving up for another Saturday night.

He dug his fingers into the base of my scalp and I moaned. "Right there." It felt as if my neck were on fire. I stared at his profile. A daughter of ours would be destined for rhinoplasty.

He leaned over and kissed my forehead, then sighed, letting his hand fall heavily to his side. "I've got a proposal," he said and kicked off his loafers. My heart skidded to a halt.

Jimmy raised himself to a sitting position. So did I. I remembered how excited I'd been a month ago when I read how Berkeley author Ayelet Waldman proposed to her husband Michael Chabon in her sleep. He reminded her of her mumblings the next morning, asked if the offer was indeed good, then accepted. If she could do it, then why couldn't I?

"I propose we relax for a while, go to Galatoires for dinner, then we'll hit Harrah's for some Blackjack." Jimmy yawned and rotated his neck in circles.

He crawled across the bed and retrieved the remote from the nightstand. Somewhere on this Saturday afternoon, there was a football game that required his attention. The headboard creaked as he leaned against it. He pulled his reading glasses from his pocket and pushed a few buttons. The roar of the crowd filled the silence.

"That's fine," I finally said. "But I've got my own proposal: How about we get married, you move to California
since you're talking about retiring anyway, we have a baby,
and, if you really want to, when my boys finish high school,
we'll move back to Louisiana?"

There! You've done it. My elation lasted a half-second before
panic took its place. Jimmy set down the remote and returned
his glasses to his pocket. He looked at me as if I'd spoken in
Cantonese. I imagined him sitting in a bar with all his buddies laughing hysterically about how this woman who he's seen
now three times in twenty years proposed to him. They'd say,
"Isn't that the Etienne girl who was the Mardi Gras queen back
in the early 80's? Boy, hasn't she come a long way!"

Jimmy crossed his arms and said, "You still fertile?"

This wasn't exactly the reaction I'd hoped for. But it wasn't
a no. I nodded.

"Me too. At least I haven't been snipped."

We both giggled. When he stopped laughing, I waited for
him to say something else. I felt silly sitting on the edge of the
mattress by myself while he leaned against the headboard. We
should have been holding hands and professing our love.

"Come here," he said and patted the nearby pillow. I walked
around the bed and sat beside him. He placed his hands on my
face and squeezed my cheeks together. Unpleasantly pinched
in his grip, I could hardly breathe. This wasn't how Michael
Chabon reacted. Was this some tribal mating ritual Jimmy
had read about in National Geographic?

Finally, he released me and said, "Lady, you're something else." Then he removed my glasses and set them on the
night stand. He looked back at me and I smiled nervously.
Yes? No? Does any part of my proposal, given that we've now

established our fertility, sound appealing? I prayed for my Michael Chabon moment.

The longer he stared without speaking the more my insecurities began a free-for-all. I fiddled with my rings, straightened my blouse, glanced at the painting of Louis Armstrong on the wall. When I couldn't stand it any longer, I said, "I don't expect an answer right away. Think about it." I kissed his nose.

He nodded and looked grateful I'd let him wiggle off the hook. Then his lips approached mine and I braced myself. His tongue swept across my teeth. I guess this would be the consolation poke. As he delved deeper into my mouth, I swore I could hear my mother asking why I hadn't chosen someone with a little more backbone.

We made love to the sounds and blinking colors of the TV. I wondered if there was a chance he'd say yes, and if so, what I'd tell my boys. I wasn't sure I wanted to start over again with another baby. Diapers. Colic. Teething. But I'd always dreamed of having a daughter. And what about my writing? My diving? Softball? I tried to imagine myself nine-months pregnant and swinging a bat. *Erectile dysfunction* . . . Some disembodied voice was endorsing that little blue pill that had put smiles on so many faces, mine as well when I looked at my stock portfolio. I hoped Jimmy wouldn't come before I did. Oh well, next time.

• • •

THE FOLLOWING EVENING, Jimmy and I kissed goodbye at the New Orleans airport. As the jet rose into the sky, my hopes plummeted. Jimmy hadn't brought up the subject of my proposal and I was too embarrassed to ask a second time. Ayelet Waldman had a law degree from Harvard. She wrote books, popped out babies, made it all look so easy. Anyone would see that she was a smart catch. I didn't have anything to offer Jimmy that he couldn't find in Louisiana.

By the time the plane began its descent into Oakland, my crushed ego had begun healing and my outlook had lifted. Jimmy had already survived two failed marriages. He needed time to sort out his feelings. He hadn't said no. There was still hope. And if I hadn't asked, hadn't risked my pride, then I'd never be in a situation to receive his answer. At least I'd sought something I truly wanted, something I'd wished for so many times when we'd dated long ago and he'd mentioned the idea. If he rejected me, then at least I'd be content knowing I tried. And if this was just a fling, I'd learned things about myself that even Jimmy couldn't take away: I'm capable of loving a man. It's not over for me yet. I'm not frigid (as my divorce had left me fearing).

The next day, I sent Jimmy a card: "I hope you'll consider my proposal. I realize you'd have to give up a lot but I also think you'd gain a lot in return. Let me know what you think."

Over the next several days, I checked my e-mail constantly, praying to see his name in my inbox. And he did e-mail but he never mentioned my card. When he finished reading *Storkbites*, he wrote to say he admired my courage and to let him know when I was in town. I took this as a good sign.

In October, I arrived in my hometown for the first of two weekends full of book signings. My memoir had become the latest big scandal in Lafayette. Jimmy offered his house and his bed as refuge and I accepted.

I woke on Saturday morning to: "What's up, cousin?" and followed the sound of Jimmy's voice. He sat at the kitchen counter talking on his cell phone. The coffee-stained newspaper had been pulled apart and folded into quarters. As I sat down, he slid the Local Interest section toward me, and pointed to an article about *Storkbites*. His bushy eyebrows shot up. His brow wrinkled.

"She's reading it right now," he said to the caller.

The article quoted my sisters and me. Some were supportive of my book, one was angry and disputed unspecified parts of my story, others had refused comment. While I read, cringing at the thought I may have caused a permanent rift in my family, I also tried to follow Jimmy's conversation. There was talk about running the boats, getting them ready for the hunting season, taking a ride out to Cypermort Point.

"I'll have to check with Ma-ree first," he said. "See what she's got going on . . ."

I grabbed a pad and pen from a nearby tray and wrote: Jimmy can go out to play. I'll take care of myself. Then I slid the note next to his coffee mug.

He took the pen from my hand and scribbled, Hush.

Score one for Marie, I thought, remembering the constant tug-of-war between his friends and me in college. When he snapped the phone shut, we settled on a compromise. He'd take me out for Mexican food then I'd run errands and visit my sister who had not returned my calls in days, while he met up with his pals. We'd reconnect for dinner after my book signing. In bed that evening, I folded myself into Jimmy's comforting arms and thought about my sister. At her kitchen table, I'd listened to her tell me how disgusted she was with me and my book. An acquaintance told her I'd asked Jimmy to marry me. "What's wrong with you?" she said. Jimmy still hadn't mentioned my proposal. I was too depressed to call him on his indiscretion or ask him whether he had an answer.

By Saturday evening of the second weekend, I figured I'd given him enough time. Although the book signings had gone well, I was exhausted, emotionally and physically. I just wanted to retreat to California and resume my version of a normal life. But before I did, I deserved a yes or a no. In his bedroom, I watched him slide off his sweat pants and turn off the lamp. Zeus' nails were clicking on the cement outside. Jimmy pulled back the blankets and scooted next to me. With my head resting on his chest, I inhaled his cologne, perhaps for the last time.

"Turns out someone isn't as discreet as they claim to be," I said.

"What do you mean?" he asked, lifting strands of my hair then letting them fall. The wine and pasta seemed to have made him drowsy. His words were thick and heavy.

"My sister heard about my proposal. Said it's all over town. Since I haven't told anyone in Louisiana, including my family, I figure that just leaves you."

"Ma-ree, I didn't tell anyone."

"Don't lie."

He sighed and shifted his body. "Well . . . I guess I thought you were just goofing around at first, 'til I got your letter. Maybe I told a couple . . . "

"It's fine. It doesn't really matter who knows now." I swallowed and squeezed my eyes shut. "Do you have an answer for me? Or is your silence your answer. If it's no, that's okay. I'm a big girl. I just need to know."

He drew me closer, and I bit my lip to keep from crying.

"I really like you, Ma-ree," he said. "You're one of the few people in this town that still manages to surprise me. But I'm not ready to pack it up and move to California." He pronounced California like Arnold Schwarzenegger and we both laughed. Several of his recent e-mails had included the line, "Give my regards to Arnold."

"I've been spending time with this woman I've known for a while," he said. "We had a sort of cooling off period but it looks like we're back on again."

I swallowed hard. Cooling off period? Is she a woman or a car? The fact that there was someone else made sense. He should have told me this when I asked if his offer of letting me stay at his house was still good. Maybe he felt like I was in a bind and he just wanted to help out an old friend.

"I hope I didn't give you the wrong impression regarding us having a long-term, long-distance relationship." He untangled his legs from mine. "I'm still messed up when it comes to women, so if I screwed up, I apologize. It's important to me that you know I have a lot of respect for you."

Does this respect mean he'd washed his sheets since Miss Cooling Off slept over?

"I wouldn't have spent the time we did recently if that were not the case," he said. "You're a special person with a lot of courage, more than I have, and I hope you find what you're looking for in a man."

I lay there feeling numb, disappointed, confused, and . . . relieved. Yes, relieved. I'd almost injected my boys and me with a lethal dose of chaos. At least Jimmy had the sense to say no. He couldn't change who he was. It was time for me to find a partner who was the opposite of Jimmy, someone stable, someone I could depend on. I no longer wanted to be one of those women who stood on the littered curb and traded her affections for trinkets.

"Are you done?" I asked. "Or is there more to your speech?"

He leaned away from me and looked directly into my face. I smiled. I wasn't angry. He nodded. "Done."

"I appreciate your candor," I said. "I knew the whole proposal thing was a long shot. The thing is, I've always loved you. I'm glad you were part of my life. Yet some day, I hope someone, a nice man, will show up at my door in California and he'll be ready for me. I hope that the stars, moon, and whatever the third thing is do align for you. I hope you get that baby you want." I took a deep breath.

"The sun."

"What? Oh, yes. The sun."

"I love you, too."

I held on to his sweet words, knowing that was the most I could hope for with him.

WHAT LOVE
ISN'T

OVER THE YEARS, experience has taught me a lot about what romantic love isn't. Love isn't meeting a man in a bar, staying up with him all night snorting cocaine and discussing the minutiae of life—its beauty and struggles—as a preamble to wild monkey sex, then while stealing away from your townhouse, he grabs the crystal vase your mother gave you last Christmas to bring home to his wife. No, that's not love. Nor is it answering phone calls at 10 p.m. from a man who says, "What's doing? How about I stop by?" So he wants me to bend over. Without dinner and a movie first? Puh-lease.

Love isn't finding a deserted spot in the woods with the backdoor man who says he'd lay you at his place if he didn't have to sneak you past his girlfriend/roommate. At least he was considerate: he actually ripped off the plastic bag from his dry-cleaned suits and spread the clothing out on the grass so I wouldn't get twigs and bugs in my hair. But love? Uh . . . no.

Then there's the man who's so worried about your safety he insists you keep his gun in your underwear drawer. Yet one day you return from work to find he's been in your apartment, and taken his gun back, as well as the envelope of cash you'd saved for your first weekend trip together.

Love isn't opening your hotel door at 2 a.m. to find the married guy bearing gifts before he heads home to his wife and children.

Although love is conveyed in many different ways, it's probably safe to assume that when a man who is first getting to know you asks, "Do you shave your pussy?" he isn't really viable dating material. Not that I'm opposed to a bald kitty fetish. I just don't think it's an appropriate inquiry until at least the third date.

Is it love when your gynecologist says, "My wife is just a frigid hag and oh, you feel so good"? I'd say run if a man you've known as a platonic friend invites you to dinner when you're in LA and in an e-mail beforehand lays out his plan: "Friends is fine. But if we're to get together, I really want to *do you*. Know what I mean?"

Love is certainly not the teenage boyfriend who finally manages to slip his cock in your privates then afterwards sends you a nasty note about how you're a slut. It doesn't even approach love when a man penetrates a woman over and over, despite her pleas to stop, and then laughs the next day when she complains of her soreness.

Love is not the man who says, "I've been offered a job with full insurance benefits. Now we can get married. Would you like that?" Then when he hears that you've told your co-workers the wonderful news, and they throw an impromptu champagne and cake party at noon, he retreats. "Engaged?

What are you talking about? I didn't ask you to marry me." But as you start to cry he steps back into the batter's box. "Don't cry. I guess since you've already told them we'll get married." Then one block from City Hall on your way to get the license, two days before your wedding day, he confesses, "Forgot to tell you. I've been married before. A friend of a friend needed a green card. I'm pretty sure we filed for divorce."

Is it love to harass a woman who has told you repeatedly that she isn't interested in seeing you outside of group activities, such a softball, insisting that she give you a chance, that you've undergone a lot of therapy yourself, and would happily play the shrink to help her through her "issues"?

Love definitely isn't a man who invites a girl he scarcely knows out on a date, fucks her in a public forum when she's drunk, and then leaves her with bloody knees and ankles to sort out the mess the next morning.

What about the man who calls every day with, "Hey, gorgeous . . . Hi, beautiful," and then one stoned afternoon remarks, "From this angle you really don't look so good," or "You know you're not the kind of woman I usually date. My friends expect to see me with eye candy."

Is it love when a guy tells you constantly that he doesn't feel the same chemistry as with his prior girlfriend? Perhaps if you'd wear contacts, lose weight, change your hair style, wear different clothes . . . then he might find you attractive. And yet, this same guy doesn't understand your reluctance to spread your legs at his whim. That's really truly love, right? Okay, maybe not. But then what is it?

Maybe love is all about time, its length, breadth, and depth: how well for how long, not how much longer. The man who says, "You're not the usual deal and that's what I greatly appreciate about you." It could be the new boyfriend you've seen three or four times who calls after leaving your apartment to say, "I was hoping you'd invite me to stay over. But looks like I'll get to enjoy the anticipation a little longer."

POOR LITLE
RICH BOY

THERE IS A BLACK AND WHITE photograph paper-clipped to a letter, tucked inside a folder labeled "Daddy" that sits on my desk. The gray-haired woman in the photo is my paternal grandmother. She's sitting on a white cement bench wearing a heavy black wool coat with a fur-trimmed collar, sheared beaver perhaps. The first thing you will notice about her face are the dark eyes. Not only are the eyes themselves as black as her coat, but the lids surrounding them appear to have been smudged in charcoal. The next thing you'll spot is her pug nose. Daddy must have gotten this feature from her, and in turn, passed it down to his nine children. You can see from my grandmother's hesitant smile that two front teeth are missing. She is wearing lipstick and white earrings the size of large buttons. She is a heavy-set woman with a long torso and poised in her lap are her large pale hands. Her wrists are turned at an unnatural angle, as if her hands have atrophied.

In this photo my grandmother is sitting alone. The paint on the bench has chipped in spots and there is grass growing below her. A stone and brick institution, its windows blackened, stands stark in the background. Next you'll see that the hem of her coat, parted at the knees, reveals a fashionable white print dress with a repeated pattern of magnolia leaves. What grabs my attention now, and every time I look at this picture, is that she is wearing hosiery. Although I know very little about this woman, I would bet that when her attendants dressed her for the photograph, they knew to cover her legs.

This picture is clipped to a letter from St. Vincent's Hospital, a mental facility in St. Louis, Missouri. It is addressed to my father, signed by the director, and dated March 18, 1966. By that time my grandmother had been a patient for thirty plus years.

Dear Mr. Etienne,

I am enclosing the pictures taken of your mother. At least these are the ones that she liked the best and thought should be sent to you. Unfortunately, she had some teeth extracted shortly before your request. Some of the pictures of her smiling showed this and she didn't like them.

One of my six sisters found this letter in Daddy's files after his death in 1993. By this time, his mother had also died. As my father put it on the rare occasions he spoke of her, she had come down with a bad case of the "baby blues" shortly after giving birth to him. Unlike postpartum depression, her baby blues didn't go away.

My paternal grandfather was a prominent wholesale druggist in New Iberia. He met my grandmother, a wealthy woman in St. Louis, married her and brought her back to Louisiana.

They set up house on Main Street and had a healthy son, my father. But quickly it became apparent that something was not right. She cried at the slightest comment, and expressed bizarre ideas, some suicidal. In public, her erratic behavior drew stares.

In 1932, the drugs we have today to manage mental illness were not available to treat schizophrenia. My grandmother was sent away to an insane asylum. I figure my grandfather chose this particular hospital because it was closer to her parents and far enough away from him and her son to spare them the shame of local gossip. New Iberia was a small, tight-knit community. At age four, Daddy was told his mother had suddenly died. He was too young to suspect a lie or wonder why there wasn't a funeral.

Daddy grew up under the care of his father and aunt. Although he spoke infrequently about his past, when he did I listened carefully. He said his mother was an accomplished pianist and had a lovely voice. She was vivacious, tall, slender, and very striking, the physical description consistent with the one photo of her displayed in his study. My father said his lonely childhood was why wanted to have so many children.

Daddy hated wide porches and tall ceilings of old houses like the one he grew up in. They were cold and drafty, too many rooms to get lost in. Around the time he decided to sell the last of his family's properties in New Iberia, I was dating Jimmy. I begged Daddy to let me buy the house so I could renovate and live in it after college, but he refused, saying New Iberia wasn't the place for me. He never encouraged my curiosity about his hometown, he never showed much enthusiasm for any of the offspring of his classmates—even those I dated or ran around with.

Daddy was left to fend for himself much of his childhood. As a result, he became fond of Campbell's Soups. One of his first investments in the stock market was in the Campbell's company. "Common sense," he said. "I figured people everywhere, like me, had discovered this meal in a can."

Family lore has it that Daddy continued to believe his mother was dead until after his sixteenth birthday. Perhaps my grandfather had meant to tell the truth, eventually. I'd like to believe he was a decent man. Maybe he felt an explanation would be more meaningful, less painful, after his son matured. Or perhaps the lie became increasingly complicated.

A doctor from St. Vincent's telephoned asking for Chester Etienne. At this point, my grandfather's alcoholism had left him virtually incompetent. He was running the family business into debt and his mental faculties were severely compromised. Without thinking that the man on the phone might mean Chester Senior, my father said, "This is he." The man introduced himself as one of the doctors taking care of Mrs. Etienne.

"But sir," my father said, "there must be a mistake. My mother passed away twelve years ago." After confirming a few details about the family, it became clear that the doctor had the right number. Daddy's mother was not dead. She was living in an asylum. In the dozen years since her admission, her condition had not greatly improved. Now the doctors were experimenting with a new operation, a lobotomy. But they needed the family's consent.

My father always said that he himself, at sixteen years old, authorized the hospital to perform the procedure. I always thought this was odd that they'd allow a child to make such a decision, but I never dared question Daddy.

It wasn't until the next year, after the lobotomy had been performed, and after Daddy and Momma, seventeen and sixteen, had eloped to Galveston, that they took the train to St. Louis to visit my grandmother. The only thing my father ever said about this visit was that he'd never go back. And he never did. Not until his mother's funeral decades later.

On the night we buried Daddy, Momma added to the story. We were sitting in the living room trying to lift her spirits with a bottomless glass of vodka and Diet Coke. She wasn't much more forthcoming about her childhood than my father, yet tonight she began reminiscing and no one dared interrupt her. She first told us about the elopement. In a hurry to get out of New Iberia, my father had stolen a bicycle off Main Street and told Momma to hop on the handle bars. They caught a train to Galveston with only the coins he had in his piggy bank—nickels and dimes he'd saved from working at the family drug wholesale. Once they were married, they sent a wire home asking for money in lieu of wedding gifts. Then my father returned to college and my mother got a retail job, giving up her scholarship. Within a year my oldest sister was born and my parents decided to visit my grandmother.

During their brief visit, the only time Mrs. Etienne addressed her new daughter-in-law was to say, "How peculiar, my dear. You're not wearing any hosiery." For fifty years, my mother never forgave her mother-in-law for making her feel poor.

When I first read the letter from St. Vincent's Hospital, I wondered what motivated my father to request a photograph of his mother after twenty-one years. He swore he'd never visit her again and he kept his promise. In April 1966, a month after my father received the photo and letter, my mother made her first suicide attempt. Perhaps her increasingly erratic behavior made him curious about his mother's own condition.

...

IN MY CHILDHOOD, Christmas was a bittersweet time. Daddy loved all the gifts and merriment as much as any of us kids. In addition to all the items we included on our wish lists, he'd comb through catalogs to find one-of-a-kind doll houses, new electronic gadgets, matching holiday pendants for his daughters and wife, unique toys, chocolates, candies. But the holiday also seemed to stir up painful memories. In the early years, Momma played carols on the piano. Sometimes we'd all be gathered around the keyboard and suddenly my father would sob. Momma's playing, Daddy would say, had reminded him of his mother. Or we'd be ecstatically ripping open all our new presents, when we'd notice that our father had gone quiet, sitting on the sofa in his blue pajamas, a cigarette burning in his owl ashtray, a cup of steaming coffee on the end table. His chin would wobble. He'd remove his dark-framed glasses, hang his head and cry.

The first time I remember this happening there'd been no lead up, no drunken argument, no name calling. No one had been injured. "Why's Daddy crying?" I asked.

"Shu," one of my siblings said, as Momma walked over to Daddy, and without a word, set her hand on his shoulder.

It wasn't long before I learned mental illness had plagued my family for generations. Both my parents took medicine for their chemical imbalances, depressions, mood swings. One of my siblings struggled mightily her entire adult life. In our family, the signs occurred in the late teens or early twenties. As a result, I spent much of my childhood in anticipation, dread, denial; my early adulthood in fear, vigilance, denial; then as my twenties waned, and it appeared I'd eluded the legacy, I was grateful. But when my forties arrived, I learned I hadn't escaped unscathed.

• • •

I'VE ALWAYS BEEN A SNOOPER. I love things old and tucked away, forgotten, misplaced. One day in high school, I was rummaging through a cabinet in the den. There were dusty novels and children's books, some dating back to the late 1800's with endearments from family members scribbled in pencil on the inside covers. I pulled two small volumes from the heap, and said to myself, "Holy shit." Since I knew Momma was in the kitchen preparing dinner (Jim Nabors was crooning on the kitchen stereo), and she probably wouldn't be coming to the back of the house anytime soon, I headed straight to Daddy's study.

He smiled as I entered the room. "Hey, Sweetheartsabean."

"Look what I found."

I'm not sure if he immediately recognized the two books I gave him. He set the tattered one with a toddler painted on its cover in his lap, and opened the second, a photo album.

"That was you with your mother, wasn't it?" I said.

He nodded and flipped to the next page.

"She was really pretty. Look at your little knickers. You were so cute." I giggled until I realized the mood in the room had shifted. My ex-mother-in-law once told me she could always tell when her deceased husband was entering one of his depressions. He'd wake up in the morning with a grey cast to his face. That was how my father looked.

Quickly, he shut the photo album and turned a few pages of the journal his mother had kept of his first two years. He cleared his throat a couple of times but didn't say a word. She'd chronicled everything: his first gifts (gold coins, silver cups and spoons, linens, a pink silk coat), his first picture, first tear, first kiss, first creeping, first smile, first journey, first hair cut, first tooth, first laugh, first shoes (smoked elk skin with hard soles), first Christmas, first word, first step. There were no such records of my brothers and sisters and me.

Daddy set the book aside. His shoulders began rising and falling.

"Bump, you want another drink before . . ." I whipped around and there was Momma walking into the study. "What's going on?" she asked and looked at me.

"I, I . . . thought he might like to see some pictures of his mother."

"Put those away," she said and picked up Daddy's empty glass.

I removed the keepsakes from his lap and hurried out of study to my bedroom. If he didn't want the books, I would keep them. If he ever asked, which I knew he wouldn't, I'd give them back. But I wanted to have some piece of my grandmother—to know this woman who wasn't quite right, who felt emotions too deeply. I needed these snapshots of my father as a happy toddler. I sat on my bed and read an entry from her journal: "Rain, rain, little Chester wants to play," one of Daddy's first sayings. I smiled.

Then I opened the album. There were nineteen pictures.

In one photo, a chubby toddler points a hose at his mother. Standing in the garden in a modest two-piece swim suit, her head is turned to avoid the spray. The boy's soft brown curls are wet. His jumper is soaked and drooping. You can almost hear his squeals as he chases his mother around the azalea bushes. I imagined his father chuckling in the background, snapping the photo.

That Daddy felt safe enough to play like this with his mother told me a lot about their bond. I can't see a time when I would have ever done the same. Such disrespect would have meant waking up in the middle of the night to a blinding light, my mother storming across the room, her nails on my arms as she jerked me out of my bed. "Pull down your panties." It would have meant a bare-bottom spanking for not only me, but my sister as well, since we shared a room and my mother would reason that she'd also likely done something in the day to warrant a little extra discipline.

In one snapshot, Daddy's standing very close to his mom. He is wearing a white wool coat that sharply contrasts the flock of brown hens circling them on some farm. His mother holds out a piece of bread but he doesn't seem to notice.

The final photo is of my grandfather reading the newspaper. He doesn't look up to smile for the camera. The remaining black pages of the album are empty.

• • •

WHEN *STORKBITES* FIRST came out in 2003, I received e-mails from extended family, former classmates, old boyfriends, and surprisingly, friends of my parents. The letters that began with, "I am a childhood friend of your father . . ." I read with a sense of dread. I feared they'd scold me for bringing shame on my deceased parents and our family. Each note I received immediately sparked guilt. After all, I had pulled aside the curtains and let people peek in the windows to see the physical and verbal fights between my parents, the beatings of the children, the drunken rages, the cruelties my siblings and I inflicted on each other, the suicide attempts, my brother's murder and its grim aftermath, my crazed promiscuity, drinking and drug use, failed marriage, struggles with my sons.

I envy anyone who doesn't worry about how he or she is perceived by others. It seems so often my own self-worth hangs on the opinions of outsiders. To my shock and relief, the letters about my book were kind, often flattering. One man wrote to say that he was in the Cub Scouts with Daddy. He and his wife invited me to lunch whenever I was in town again so that we could trade stories about my father. We corresponded a couple of times before I got up the nerve to ask him something I'd fretted over for decades: "Did everyone in New Iberia know that my father's mother had been sent away to an asylum? Or did they believe, as he had, that she'd died when he was four? Were there rumors?"

Daddy had gone around unaware, playing the King of the Mardi Gras ball, donning his Cub Scouts uniform with all those cute little patches, debating with the debate team, tooting "When the Saints Come Marching In" on his horn, and then one day he learned that he'd been living a farce.

The last thing I wanted was for people to look too closely at me, see I was damaged, and laugh. I'm sure my father had felt ostracized, isolated from everyone, including his family.

His friend replied:

Dear Marie,

Growing up I did know from my parents that Chester's mother was living in an institution in St. Louis. It was all very hush-hush. I never talked with Chester about that and did not know that he had been told she was dead. The fact that the mother was in an institution, although Chester Senior may have made an effort to keep it under wraps, was general knowledge in the community.

I believe that Chester Senior did not know what to do with his little boy. People in town thought of Chester as a "poor little rich boy," since his mother had been taken away and his father and aunt could afford to give him anything he wanted.

A neighbor knew Chester's mother and says that she was taken away without explanation when Chest was four.

They may have been able to "afford" to give him anything he wanted, but . . . I doubt it.

MURDER?
SUICIDE?

I WAS SITTING IN MY stockbroker's office in Lafayette with Mr. Delahoussaye, our family's long-time accountant, and Ken, the financial planner who helped manage my trust. We were discussing their reactions to *Storkbites* when Mr. D said, "I'm surprised you portrayed Chess as being murdered. I always heard it was suicide."

"Why would Chess commit suicide?" I asked Mr. D, surprised by my angry tone. My younger brother Nickey definitely killed himself—at age nineteen (same age as Chess when he died) in my parents' bedroom, with Daddy's gun. My parents drank themselves to death. My mom's mother starved herself . . . but Chess? Suicide? No way. He was murdered.

He shrugged and looked across the desk at Ken, who had been my father's broker and friend.

"I heard the same thing . . . suicide," Ken said. He glanced down at the Excel spreadsheets he'd prepared and seemed eager to review. "I didn't know your dad personally then, but the story I heard was that the oldest Etienne son had over-dosed on drugs over the breakup of some girl."

"Baloney. Chess wouldn't have killed himself over a girl. And if it wasn't murder, why would there have been those investigations? All those strange people calling our house? Why would Daddy have hired a guard and sent Chess's tissue samples to his friend at NASA?"

Mr. Delahoussaye shrugged again. "Darling, you might be right. That was one subject your dad never talked about with me. But those were the rumors."

"Didn't Chess work at the wholesale for a time?" I said. "Did he seem unhappy? Suicidal?"

Mr. Delahoussaye said, "Your brother was full of spunk. He was a bundle of nervous energy. Sometimes he'd get so restless filling orders in the warehouse, like a gorilla ready to attack in his cage, I'd ask one of the drivers to take him on deliveries. The doctors and nurses loved him. He made them laugh. But he had some problems."

Ken cleared his throat. "Shall we?" He passed out the spreadsheets and graphs. Enough family reminiscing, it was time to get the meeting underway.

Afterwards, I shook hands with Ken and hugged Mr. Delahoussaye good-bye. Before going back to my sister's to check on my boys, I drove through Greenbriar Subdivision, our old neighborhood. Winding my way along West Bayou Parkway, I looked at the occasional For Sale signs, trying to remember which family lived in which house when I was growing up. The vacant, oak-studded lots surrounding our house, lots where we played softball and held our yard sales, were now filled with colossal brick and stucco homes and non-native plants. Palm trees in Louisiana? Birds of Paradise?

Each family seemed determined to outdo its neighbors.

As our old home came into view, I considered my conversation with Mr. Delahoussaye and Ken. Perhaps it didn't matter, but their belief, one apparently shared by others in the community, that my older brother Chess had committed suicide, bothered me tremendously. It wasn't a matter of feeling ashamed or culpable in some way, but I wondered if Chess would have been so hurt, so cruel even as to grant Momma's wish. The night before he was found abandoned in a ditch off the old highway between Lafayette and New Iberia, he and my mother had an ugly fight. This one didn't get physical, as some did, but in her drunken rage she screamed how she hated him and wished he'd die.

Perhaps my memory was flawed but not once did I recall hearing the word "suicide" spoken in the same breath as Chess's name. I'd eavesdropped at the door of the piano room on Daddy and his friends when they talked privately about the investigation. I'd hovered nearby when he made calls on the newly installed private line in his workshop. No one said suicide.

My brother's murder, and the violence and mystery surrounding it, had become part of my identity. Before Chess's death, I was a sweet, mischievous nine-year-old girl who, in many ways, was happy. I had a big house with lots of toys, a fancy swimming pool with a slide, lots of siblings to play with, a handsome father whom I adored and who always brought home strange state-of-the-art gadgets, and a mother who, when she wasn't washing my mouth out with Lava soap, pulling me out of bed to spank, or hitting me with a hairbrush, was reassuringly predictable, preparing three meals each and every day and ensuring that we always had enough clothes and shoes. But from July 4, 1971 on, I became the girl whose older brother, the one who played the drums and told gory stories, left for breakfast one morning and never returned. No one else I knew had the tissue samples of her dead brother stored in the deep freeze with yellow police tape barring entry. Only my closest friends knew we had an off-duty officer living with us at night during the months-long investigation. Yes, I was now different than my peers. My brother, according to hushed conversations, had been murdered. I was angry and scared and I was special.

For years after Chess's death I gathered information. My father often told his closest friends that he believed drugs were slipped into Chess's drink at a roadside bar, although subsequent autopsies wouldn't verify any such thing. All we really knew was that my brother left the bar with some acquaintances, including the maid who worked for a nearby family. They drove him a short distance before ejecting him from the car into a ditch, where he was spotted lying unconscious. I heard my father say that he knew who these people were who killed his son but he couldn't prove it. The words spewed out of his mouth like rusty razor blades.

I felt incredible rage toward whoever had brought my powerful father to his knees. Despite all his money, access to shady characters who could take care of anything outside the usual routes, he couldn't bring my brother's killer to justice.

At nine, ten, eleven . . . I was the girl looking for clues to solve the crime. I adopted the most widely believed story about Chess's death: He was killed by drug suppliers who feared he'd turn them in after a large stash of pot was found in his car following an accident. It didn't really matter why the so-called killers thought he'd betray them. I had all the proof I needed. The same day Chess died, our white rabbit, LaPay, disappeared, and I was told by my older sisters that the killers transfused LaPay's blood to Chess. Maybe to cover drugs that could be traced to them, maybe for the joy of confusing the police, maybe because the ceremony had even more sinister implications. Any of these reasons made as much sense as any other. This was Louisiana.

When the local coroner failed to find traces of drugs and couldn't determine the cause of death, Daddy shipped the tissue samples to his friend at NASA for an independent analysis.

Now, thirty-two years later, I stopped at the curb of our old brick house on Woodvale and wondered if the current owners ever have the misfortune of running into Chess's ghost as I had as a child.

A few months after my brother's death, three of my sisters and I were having a sleepover with a close family friend, playing cards on my bed, when two of us looked at the window. Our shrieks set off the others and soon we were all screaming. My father, half asleep, raced into my room in his wrinkled pajamas.

"Chess!" I cried. "I saw Chess in the window! I think he was in hell."

My friend still clutched my arm. "I saw him too, Mr. Etienne. He was in flames. The whole window was on fire."

I nodded and quickly glanced at the window fearing I'd see my brother's fiery face again. There was nothing there but the reflection of four hysterical girls.

"Your brother's not in hell. Now go to sleep," Daddy said, without looking at the window.

Remembering this now as I stared at the empty carport, I wondered that if Chess had been murdered, wouldn't I have seen him in heaven? Raised Catholic, I believed at the time that hell was for people who either committed suicide or did horrible deeds while living. I knew Chess was no saint—he drank a lot, cussed at Momma, even kicked her stomach once when she was pregnant with Nickey—but were these sins serious enough to bar him from heaven? Why had the idea of suicide not entered my mind? Or had it and I just refused the notion because it didn't jibe with my new world?

There was a night about three years after Chess's death, when the Duhons, my parents' closest friends, pulled into our driveway in their massive Lincoln. Just as Daddy and Momma climbed out of the car, my sister pulled in beside them. She threw the station wagon into park and followed me and my other sister as we ran toward Daddy.

"Fun evening," Daddy said to the Duhons as he waved good-bye. Momma probably added something like, "Come for happy hour tomorrow." That was the standing invitation.

"Hey, Sweetheartsabean," Daddy said. "What's going on? Is somebody hurt?"

Sobbing, I threw my arms around him and buried my face in his suit jacket. "We don't want you to die," I said. "Don't let those people kill you too."

My sisters, also crying, huddled close. "We're so scared, Daddy. What if they come after you?"

"Everything all right, Chester?" Mr. Duhon called out. He was standing by his car.

He ignored Mr. Duhon's question, pried loose my arms, and scowled. "No one is going to kill me."

"You were talking on the phone this afternoon," I said. "You said someone wants ten thousand dollars." I sniffled. "I heard you say that you were scared they'd come after you if you didn't pay them."

"No, Sweetheartsabean—"

A siren cut off his words. Two seconds later, a city patrol car, lights flashing, pulled into the driveway, blocking Mr. Duhon's Lincoln.

Mr. Duhon approached. "Chester, what's going on?"

Instead of answering his friend, Daddy offered his hand to the first officer. "Chester Etienne. Can I help you?"

The policemen introduced themselves. The passenger door to the Lincoln opened and Mrs. Duhon spilled out of the car. "Chester, are the children all right?" she slurred.

"We'd like a word with you," one officer said. "Your daughters said you've received some threats. They're worried about your safety."

Daddy rubbed his stubble, his cheeks were pink from a night of Jack Daniels. He sighed. "They've got very active imaginations," he said, sounding strangely casual, even smiling at the men.

I'd felt so empty at that moment when Daddy dismissed us with those words: *very active imaginations.* I had wanted to protect him. I didn't want anyone to take him away like they had my brother. It wasn't only that I loved my father, but now that Chess was gone, Daddy was the only buffer, no matter how slight, between us and Momma. If he was gone, we'd be at her mercy, day and night.

Daddy told the Duhons to go on home and for us to go up to our rooms. He and Momma led the officers into the study. I sat in bed and listened and wondered how much trouble I'd gotten myself into. About twenty minutes later the dog barked, there were footsteps across the brick floor, the back door closed, the gate slammed shut, an engine roared. I peered out my window and watched the police car back out of the driveway. Someone scooped ice, water ran through the pipes, stairs creaked under the weight of footsteps. Daddy's throat cleared and I scooted against the headboard as my door opened.

"Just wanted to say good-night," he said and crossed the room somberly, his shoulders slumped. It appeared the unexpected visit had sobered him up.

"I'm sorry we talked to those policemen," I mumbled.

"It's okay. But no one's going to harm me. I don't want you to worry anymore. Do you understand?"

I nodded. "I love you, Daddy."

"I love you too, Sweetheartsabean." He bent over, kissed me gently on the forehead, and then smoothed the blanket. "Sleep tight and don't let the bed bugs bite." It had been years since he'd tucked me in with those words.

Every time I believed our family had moved on, some new event would reopen the wounds. I returned from school one afternoon to find Daddy's car under the carport. He was home early, which was very unusual back then. I walked into the kitchen and immediately noticed there was nothing on the stovetop or in the oven. In the den, Momma wasn't on the sofa watching the end of her soaps. The hall door leading to the study was closed. Something was up.

That evening, I learned Daddy hadn't returned to the office after lunch. One of my older sisters told me the maid said she'd been folding clothes in the laundry room when she heard the back door open. Knowing Daddy was napping and the rest of us were at school or running errands, she went to see who it was. There, standing in the kitchen, was a young man she swore was Chess. Her scream woke Daddy, who came running from the study.

Daddy gripped the edge of the table and asked, "Is that you, son?" The man, my brother, whoever it was, said something to him (I never learned what exactly) then turned and left. Daddy broke down and the maid gave her notice. Of course, Daddy never talked about any of this with us. He was like a child we had to protect by not upsetting him.

Murder? Suicide? I want to blame someone for my brother's death. I want to know that unhappiness doesn't, ultimately, have to end in suicide (or murder).

WHERE THE LINES
CONVERGE

AFTER DADDY'S DEATH in 1993, with my mother's permission, I gathered his art supplies—sketchbooks, how-to books, a briefcase filled with tubes of oil paints and sable brushes—and brought them back to California with me. It wasn't until my son Zack was preschool age and wanted to learn how to use the feather he'd found on the school playground as a writing instrument that I opened one of the sketchbooks.

There on the yellowed paper was my father's distinctive printing. It always looked like someone took his words and stretched them out horizontally. In caps, neatly and properly spaced, was the following definition:

LINEAR PERSPERBPECTIVE: USING THE RIGHT AND LEFT VANISHING POINT—THAT IMAGINARY POINT WHERE ALL THE LINES <u>SEEM</u> TO CONVERGE.

To demonstrate, he'd sketched a house with lines shooting off the corners of the walls and the roof to the left and right margins. Two small dots denoted where all the lines converged. I noticed that he'd misspelled perspective and laughed to myself. Daddy with his genius IQ was a stickler for proper grammar.

Zack sat beside me at the dining room table and said, "We ready yet?" Austin, six, joined us to watch.

"One second, sweetie." I flipped through the pages of notes and rough sketches he used as studies for his paintings. These notes, as always, were written in black felt pen. After turning to a fresh page, I opened the bottle of ink and dipped the tip of the feather. "Just like magic," I said and drew a smiley face. "Now you've got a pen."

"Can I try it?" Zack grabbed the feather. He doodled on the page for a few minutes, re-inking the tip frequently before Austin insisted it was his turn. As my eldest son practiced writing his name, he asked, "How does the feather work?"

"It's porous. Sucks the ink right up like a sponge."

Soon the boys tired of the project and ran off to play. Alone in the dining room, I opened the sketchbook back to the first page and reread my father's words:

THAT IMAGINARY POINT WHERE ALL THE LINES <u>SEEM</u> TO CONVERGE.

Just before Daddy died, he was still taking art classes. An interest in art was our own point of convergence. It was the one hobby that for him set me apart from my eight siblings. But in high school, I started down a rebellious path that led to blackouts, wrecked cars, and teen pregnancy. It took a smashed-up Pontiac with an ice chest full of beer before my father finally noticed his wayward daughter. I presume that was when he devised his plan for us to spend more time together.

Daddy found an artist, Mrs. Babineaux, from the nearby one-stoplight town of Broussard, and told me we were going to take oil painting classes together. When I complained that I didn't have the time or interest, he refused to budge. "It's only one night a week," he insisted. "Besides, I've already paid for the lessons."

So every Wednesday night after dinner, the doorbell rang, and Daddy escorted Mrs. Babineaux to his workshop off the back of the house. Most nights I plunked down in a canvas chair in my pleated Catholic school skirt and white blouse, sighing two or three times to let them both know I felt imposed upon. Rather than surrender two precious hours to this I could have been talking on the phone to my boyfriend Dwayne or doing homework. My father, dressed in pressed khakis and an old shirt, sat beside me with an ash tray and a pack of Winstons. I squirmed in my chair, making an occasional note in my own tablet as Mrs. Babineaux rattled on about some aspect of the craft of painting. As she yammered, the windows of the workshop overlooking our swimming pool fogged up.

The evenings wore on and eventually I settled into the lessons. By the time we were allowed to select a paint brush and make our first stroke, I had stopped squirming. I lifted the needle off the This-Is-So-Stupid record playing in my head and concentrated. Sitting next to my father, smelling the scent of his aftershave and shampoo, I felt like his little girl again. Here with my father the most difficult decision I had to make was what to paint and how to execute it.

Daddy created landscapes and still lifes. I usually depicted Dwayne on and off the baseball field. Mrs. Babineaux hovered over us offering tips and encouragement. Sometimes she took the brush into her own gnarled hands and showed how adding a contrasting color, say violet or blue, would hint at something unseen, like the rocks beneath a waterfall. As the smell of cigarette smoke and turpentine filled the room, Daddy and I admired each other's progress. "Oh, my gosh, they look like real feathers," I said, wanting to touch his canvas and feel the breast of an owl he'd perched on a tree.

In one session Mrs. Bab handed Daddy a soft piece of cloth. "Use this. It's excellent for cleaning your brush." He dabbed the cloth with turpentine, then carefully wiped off the red paint. "The cotton lining from my old underwear," she announced.

Daddy dropped the piece of fabric and jerked away so fast the wooden joints of his chair let out an angry squeak. The three of us looked down at the red-smeared wad on the orange Linoleum floor. I had to stifle a laugh. My father absolutely couldn't stomach anything having to do with other people's bodily functions and this looked too much like what he'd find in a dirty clothes hamper. Mrs. Babineaux seemed unfazed. She picked up the cloth—"Let's not waste this"—and tossed it into her paper bag.

After Mrs. Bab's noisy car backed out of our driveway, I said, "Wasn't that underwear thing gross," and wrinkled my nose for emphasis.

My father chuckled and shook his head. "What a kook!"

He put his arm around me as we walked to the back door. I was so happy. Our hearts had temporarily converged.

• • •

Midway into my art lessons with Daddy, Dwayne began pressuring me to attend a series of LSU fraternity parties with him. He was going off to college the next year and the frats were courting him. I'd asked my father for permission several times and each time he'd say, "You're not going to Baton Rouge for the weekend. You're only sixteen."

"I promise to sleep in the girls' dorm." One of my sisters had friends who lived on campus.

"No!"

"I swear I'll call each evening so you'll know I'm in for the night."

"No!"

Before I asked again, I waited until after dinner so my parents had consumed enough cocktails to be in a receptive mood but not enough to have slid down the back side of the bottle. I stood in the study between their recliners and presented the latest proposal that Dwayne and I had thought up.

"What if we stayed at Dwayne's older brother and sister-in-law's house in Baton Rouge," I said. "We'll be in by midnight. I'll give you their phone number if you want to check on us."

"Absolutely not," my father said.

My mother sipped her vodka and Tab. She must have decided to sit out this argument. I searched for another angle. My father's landscape paintings hung behind his chair next to a metal sculpture of an owl. Before I considered the consequences, I said, "I'll quit taking art with you."

His brown eyes looked as black as the rims of his glasses. He stared at me for a moment then turned toward the television. His feet twirled in circles as he did when he was angry. He reached for his drink, still no response. As he brought the tumbler to his lips, he mumbled, "My answer is still no."

"I . . . I . . . I'm serious. No more lessons with that stupid lady."

He took a gulp of his Jack Daniels, then carefully set his drink on the marble side table. With the back of his hand he wiped his lips. "That's a darn shame. Guess we're done here."

I stormed out, my heart pounding. What just happened in there? How do I undo this? I pictured myself running back into the study: "Won't you at least negotiate with me? Beg me not to quit our art classes?" But when it came to pride and stubbornness, my father and I were well-matched.

In an unexpected reversal a few days later, he knocked on my bedroom door and said, "Go to Baton Rouge if you want."

"Really?"

His face was set hard as he stared down at me. In that moment, I could feel that something had shifted permanently in our relationship. Was it that he no longer cared what trouble I found myself in? Even so, I thought that I should have been happy. But I wasn't.

WHEN YOUR
DAUGHTER
GETS BOOBS
AND TURNS INTO
A TRAMP

I ONCE ASKED THE FATHER of one of my fellow spring-board divers what it was like to watch his teenage daughter walk around in a bikini and flirt with boys who only a year before she and her girlfriends had considered evil. We were chums and could say these things to each other. His eyes widened. "It's like having your favorite golden retriever get boobs. Suddenly you can't cuddle up with her on the sofa anymore. You want to build a barricade around her to protect her."

Daddy tried so hard to keep my older sisters from turning into "tramps," the label Momma often hurled at them. If it took punching a boy in the nose to protect their chastity, that's what he did. But by the time his younger daughters (like me) traded in training bras for something with an actual cup, he had given up.

The summer before my freshman year of college, Daddy booked an eleven-day cruise for our family vacation. He'd gotten on the cruise kick two years before, found he enjoyed floating around the Caribbean with cocktail bars every ten feet. And the scenery was hardly objectionable: tanned, bikini-clad women bent over shuffleboard pucks. The only part of these sea vacations he detested were the comings and goings— customs in particular. Standing in long lines in Miami, especially in August, can bring out the beast in anyone.

I knew from experience that the air travel portion of a trip was serious business. Daddy's motto included pack only what you were willing to carry yourself, arrive at least two hours before the departure time (this was pre-9/11), and don't wander off to check out the airport gift shops or complain that you're bored. It didn't matter that we'd be the first travelers in the terminal or that even the Early Bird coffee shop hadn't opened yet.

The Friday evening before embarking on our big outing, I had a date with a popular jock, the older brother of one of my friends. Brian was good-looking in an opposites-attract way: brown hair and eyes versus my blond-hazel combo. I didn't know him well but this added to the excitement and anticipation.

We joined Brian's friend and his friend's girlfriend for dinner at one of my family's favorite seafood restaurants. I had worried all day what I'd say to this boy and his friends, whom I also hardly knew. It was a huge relief when the husband of my family's maid introduced himself as our waiter. I now had an ally. And as quickly as I'd finish one beer, he'd set down another.

"Weren't very hungry tonight, Miss Marie?" was all our waiter said as he removed the half-eaten crabmeat au gratin I'd anxiously nibbled. Eating in front of family and friends, much less virtual strangers, had always frightened me, especially after the mayonnaise incident.

After dinner we headed to the University of Southwestern Louisiana campus to the fraternity house that Brian had pledged. The other couple immediately joined another group of friends. Brian led me into a crowded smoke-filled room. "Wait here," he said over all the noise. "I'll get us another beer." Pace yourself, Marie. You've got a long night ahead. Don't want to end up drunk, blowing your chances with yet another guy. Soon Brian returned with two large beers. I took a sip, and tried to think of something clever to say. He looked around the room as I sipped my beer. Then everything went black.

• • •

THE NEXT MORNING my telephone buzzed me awake. At first the sound seemed part of a dream and I ignored it. When I finally fumbled for the receiver, I knocked over a coffee mug filled with pens and pencils, which rolled off the edge of the headboard into the abyss behind my bed. My head pounded.

"Marie, the car will be here in an hour," Momma said on the phone. My bedroom sat directly above the kitchen. No doubt she was standing at the sink next to an ashtray already filled with red-stained butts. "Come have breakfast, bring your suitcase."

I hung up, rolled over, and buried my throbbing head under the pillow. The lining of the bedspread scratched my legs and I winced. What the hell? Carefully, I rolled over and pulled myself up. I gaped at my knees and toes, which were scraped raw, blades of grass and gravel embedded in the wounds. What happened last night? Why was I still wearing my sundress? How did I get into . . . I flinched as I recalled the image of headlights shining straight into my eyes . . . me on my knees and hands . . . and behind me . . . I squeezed my eyes shut.

The door leading to my shared bathroom suddenly opened. My little sister entered. "You better get up. Momma and Daddy are in a *supremely* foul mood." I pulled the hem of my dress to cover my knees and hoped she wouldn't notice my feet. She informed me one of our sisters still hadn't come home from her date and hadn't bothered to call Momma and Daddy to let them know whether she was alive or lying in some ditch. Momma was now threatening to leave her behind if she didn't show up soon. "So if you don't want to find your-self in the doghouse, too, I'd get your butt in gear."

When she shut the door, a yellowed sheet of a newspa-per comic fell off the nearby wall. For months the clipping had been slowly peeling away. Now it had come completely unglued, floating down to the orange-red carpet, leaving a large gap in the collage I had put up a couple years earlier.

If my parents were on a rampage, I certainly didn't want to bring any attention to myself. My AWOL sister could have that honor. Quickly, I cleaned my scrapes with a warm wash-cloth, picked the pebbles and grass from the deeper cuts, then grabbed another towel to wash my face and between my legs. My crotch didn't feel swollen. Maybe Brian had a pinky dick. Surely if there had been other guys involved, a group hoorah, there'd be swelling. There wasn't even an odor of sex. I prayed that maybe, just maybe, I'd simply fallen down. But that really didn't fit with my injuries and the image of me on all fours.

Trying to divert my thoughts to something less frightening, I considered the dilemma of what to wear. Shorts and tennis shoes would cover my toes but not my knees. And with my cut up feet, I wasn't going to pull on a pair of socks much less tight tennis shoes. Jeans would hide my knees but would rub. I finally settled on a wraparound skirt, one with a wide hem that wouldn't brush against or show off my knees, and a pair of sandals with thin straps. I'd just try to keep my feet out of view.

I dragged my suitcase down to the foyer and added it to a half-dozen others lined up at the front door. Judging by my reflection in the huge beveled mirror, I knew that even an entire garden of cucumbers wouldn't repair the dark circles under my bloodshot eyes. Hopefully Momma and Daddy wouldn't ask why I looked so wretched and was limping.

I approached the kitchen door, then froze when Momma shouted, "It's about goddamn time," followed by Daddy's "Where the hell have you been? The limo will be here in twenty minutes. This is the last goddamn vacation I'm taking you kids on."

My sister had turned up. She wasn't dead like Chess after all. Not yet, anyway. Not wanting to get caught in the fracas, I waited and listened.

"Sorry. So and so invited me to sleep over after my date. I forgot to call you . . . "

Sleeping over at a girlfriend's house and forgetting to call: a common lie we all used. It was far more believable than, "We got lost and then the car broke down." We knew neither Momma nor Daddy would ever bother to verify the alibi, which relieved them from having to address an awkward situation like a daughter's promiscuity and out-of-control drinking.

"Just go get ready and be down here with your luggage in fifteen minutes," Daddy said. "Do you hear me?"

I stepped out of my sister's way as she raced to the stairs.

Approaching the kitchen table, I said, "Good morning, Daddy." Already dressed in a dark grey suit, his tie flung over his right shoulder, he leaned over a plate of buttered grits and bacon. I bent down and kissed his freshly shaven cheek, which smelled familiarly of Old Spice.

"Did you bring your suitcase down?" he said without looking up. "You didn't pack more than one?"

"Yes, sir. I'm mean, no sir. Just one." Trying to walk naturally, as though my feet weren't screaming, I headed toward the island of gas and electric stoves. "Morning, Momma."

"Come eat," she barked, releasing a mouthful of cigarette smoke. She ripped open a fresh carton of Virginia Slims and filled her enormous purse as I gave her a quick peck. There were expected customs in our family: the morning and bedtime kisses, the declarations of "I love you" upon leaving the house for school, work, a date. We'd been trained like obedient mutts to kiss and declare our love no matter how we really felt.

I served myself breakfast and plopped onto the first barstool at the counter. Even when Daddy didn't have an entire swarm of bees up his ass, I'd sit with my back to him to avoid his scrutiny. Others entered the kitchen and quietly ate their breakfast. Soon, we all piled into the limo, Daddy thankfully sitting up front with the driver. Assembled, we headed to the Lafayette airport.

Throughout the day, every time I glanced at Daddy, it seemed as if he was glaring at me over the top of his dark eyeglasses, shooting me looks of disgust and hatred: How had he ended up with a daughter like me? A slut who would let one guy after another screw her. A stupid girl with no clue about love.

As if being hung over and paranoid wasn't enough to make me wish the airplane would crash, I had to limp from airport to airport with what felt like barbed wire gnawing at my toes. My skirt stuck to the weeping cuts on my knees and whenever I pulled away the fabric, I'd find more lint embedded in the wounds. Then, no matter how hard I tried to focus on the cruise, the image of my hands and knees pressing against broken asphalt, the sensation of blinding lights, said I deserved whatever had happened in the parking lot of the Cajun Dome.

• • •

THE ONLY WAY I SURVIVED the cruise was by getting drunk and stoned with the other kids on the ship. Beer and pot temporarily obliterated the images and questions that hounded me. It took years before I could drive past the Dome without cringing.

Twenty-two years later, I called the guy with whom we double-dated that night, and asked him what happened. He was adamant nothing had been put in my drink. He said I'd simply gotten drunk. He had left Brian and me at the Cajun Dome while he took his sick girlfriend home. When he returned to the parking lot, his headlights shined on Brian and me. "Going at it," he said.

"Jesus," I whispered. "What? Did he rape me?"

"No. He wasn't forcing you—I'm sure of that."

"How . . . how could you tell?"

"A guy can tell."

"We were alone, right?"

"Guess so. Until I got there anyway."

At least there was no gang bang as I'd feared.

After the call, I thought more about the evening. I still

didn't know how I got to bed that night. Did my parents have any idea what happened to me? Have any suspicions? I've often imagined how Daddy would have reacted if I'd confided in him about the date, shared my fears, revealed my injuries. But given our family's growing need to avoid any and all unpleasantness, I of course never brought it up. I suppose if we'd had a closer father/daughter relationship, it would have been less likely, although not impossible, that I would have found myself fucking a frat boy at the Cajun Dome in the first place. If I hadn't felt so unloved, so undeserving of care and respect, maybe the date would have ended with a peck instead of a poke. And maybe, just maybe, there would have been fewer Brians in my life.

WARTS

SUPERSTITIONS. SOME ARE MUNDANE: making the sign of the cross when an emergency vehicle speeds past; knocking on wood three times to ward off bad luck; wishing on a penny. Some are borrowed: keeping a red envelope with nine pennies in my purse at all times to promote financial well-being; taking a practice swing before entering the batter's box; burying a St. Joseph statue to help me sell a house. And some are all mine: never file monthly bank statements in a red folder; always use black or blue binders for manuscripts; press the board four times before executing a back dive.

My ex-mother-in-law, an intelligent woman, had her superstitions as well. She gave a lot of credence to the power of the mind over body. From her I picked up an idea of digging a hole in my backyard, whispering my worries into the turned soil, then burying my problems to help them disappear. Once, her son developed warts all over his hands. They tried the standard drug store remedies but nothing worked. Finally, she decided to take him to the doctor. As they left the house, her son pleaded not to go. She continued to drive toward the doctor's office but allowed him one last hope. Together they prayed and chanted for the wart to be gone. When she pulled into the parking lot, her son was smiling. His voice was calm. "We don't have to see the doctor. They're gone. They've disappeared." He held up his hands and indeed they were clear of warts.

My favorite superstition, or "trick," as I've always called it, also has to do with warts. At age seven, a wart grew on the inside of my palm. I worried it constantly until one evening at dinner my father asked, "Sweetheartsabean, what are you picking at?"

Knowing he was easily repulsed, I mumbled, "A wart."

"Find a sheet of paper," he said

I trudged off to my bedroom, afraid he'd make me write lines about my bad manners—picking a wart during a meal. When I returned to the kitchen, he took the paper and removed his black felt pen and gold-plated lighter from his shirt pocket.

"Let's see your wart," he said

I turned up my palm. We both stared at the ugly growth below my left pointer finger.

He pressed my hand against the paper on the table and traced my fingers. This was how we'd drawn turkeys at school. Sandwiched between the warmth of my father's hand and the cool paper, my fingers relaxed. When he was finished, he drew a circle beneath the traced finger then folded the paper in half, and in half again.

He lit a folded corner. Just before the greedy flame devoured the copy of my hand, he dropped it into the half-full ashtray that sat next to his drink.

"When you wake, the wart will be gone," he said in a playful voice.

The next morning, I ran into the kitchen and yelled, "Daddy, Daddy! It's gone." I stuck out my hand for his inspection. "Just like you said."

"Told you." He grinned, and I hugged him. My father was the anti-mother. He was the one who could make magic.

Years later, when my younger son Zack got his first wart, he came to my room, sat on my bed, and placed his foot in my lap. I told him I'd learned a cure from my father.

"Does it hurt?"

"No, I simply burn the wart right off your foot. You won't feel much."

"Right, mom. You wouldn't do that to me."

"Get your brother and meet me in the kitchen."

I set a sheet of paper on the floor and asked Zack to step in the middle. There was skepticism in both his and Austin's face. After tracing the foot, we drew in the wart then folded the paper as my father had done.

"I get to light it," Austin said. "I'm older."

"I want to light it," whined Zack. "It's my wart."

"Each of you will light a corner."

I held the paper over the ashtray and we watched the flames consume the tracing, wart and all.

"You wait, tomorrow it will be gone."

"Yeah, right," Zack said. "This is stupid."

"You have to believe," I said. "Having faith is part of the trick."

When I kissed him good-night, he said, "I hope it works."

The next morning, Zack poked his head into my bedroom and said, "Didn't work."

We performed the ritual again that night after dinner and added a chant. "Hocus, pocus, alacazam . . ." I danced my fingers above the flame. "Let this pesky wart be gone."

"You're strange," Austin said and scooted away from me.

My father's magic didn't work for Zack as it had for me. By the end of the week, Zack's wart was the size of a plump blueberry. We made an appointment to see his pediatrician, who placed her faith in the healing powers of modern medicine.

I realize all faith is not based on superstition. Much of it is founded on trust—in yourself and others. I suppose one could find anecdotal evidence for either side of the argument—that superstitions are irrational or that they do support natural tendencies. Maybe, if someone sees a black cat and believes that misfortune awaits her around the next bush, she actually looks for that misfortune. She walks toward it. In essence, she fulfills the prophesy. Likewise, if someone truly believes in wishing on a penny, focusing her thoughts and energies on something held valuable, she may find a way to realize her dream. Perhaps believing is seeing.

A FATHER'S DAY
MOSAIC

THE PRIMARY PURPOSE of gift-giving is to create, at the very least, a momentary connection between you and another, something that says, "I know who you are. I *get* you and I *appreciate* you." Sometimes, however, the whole enterprise seems like more trouble than it's worth. I'd rather eat crickets than shop for someone who "has everything." Which brings me to my father.

After moving to California in 1986, I visited my parents in Louisiana less frequently. Without face-to-face contact, our other methods of communication became as routine as an over-rehearsed play. My mother's letters recapped their recent meals and the local gossip. Daddy and I analyzed the weather.

After my younger brother's suicide in 1986, my father steadily grew quiet. Once eccentric and high-spirited, he now seemed to be waiting for death, which, at the very least, would provide a change of scenery.

One June as Father's Day approached, I wondered what to buy for this sixty-year-old man with no interests and enough money to make a new Cadillac appear in the driveway with a mere phone call. What within my budget would stir some emotion or appreciation? Sensing I had few Father's Days remaining, I wanted to find a special gift, perhaps something from the past that once brought him pleasure and would now draw us closer.

After flipping through several photo albums, I found a picture of Daddy sitting by our swimming pool in a silly Hawaiian shirt and straw hat. He wore one of his hearty Jack Daniels smiles. I cropped the photograph along his torso, his broad shoulders, the straw hat, down the length of one arm to his tanned hand. Next, I tore sheets of construction paper into small pieces. Selecting alternate hues of blue, I glued one small piece after another onto a folded sheet of thick white paper. A mosaic of rolling waves soon covered the bottom half of the card. With the ocean in place, I positioned the brown tiles until I'd created a fishing boat, a waning crescent moon tilted on its side, but by all means seaworthy.

I dabbed glue to the backside of Daddy's photograph and set him in the middle of the craft. He smiled in his loud shirt. Life was good. The Captain, once again, his hat now providing shade from the yellow and orange mosaic sun blazing in the cloudless sky. Perfect weather for an afternoon out in the Gulf, like so many long summer days of my childhood.

But the Captain needed a challenge. I wanted to depict a battle in which Daddy was the victor, outlasting and outwitting the strongest, most determined fish. I pictured the cobalt blue marlins with their silvery bellies and spear-like jaws that hung in our house and at his office before retirement. Out of black paper, I shaped such a fish, nearly as large as my father. The fish's tail touched the tip of a wave, as if it had just been yanked from the sea. I drew a rod in Daddy's hand, the end bent toward the nose of his catch. A thin line connected the rod to the hooked mouth. Pleased with myself, I signed the card, "Happy Father's Day, Daddy. I love you."

After I sent the card (overnight express) doubts rushed in. Would he think it was funny? Childish? Would he think I was making fun of him?

"Ma-ree," Daddy said into the telephone on Saturday morning. "That's the cutest card I've ever seen. Where'd you get such an idea?"

At that moment, I was six years old again.

The conversation, as usual, was brief. After we hung up, it hardly seemed real. But when I replayed his words, heard them in the same excited voice, I knew that my gift had stirred something in him.

Monday morning, Mr. Delahoussaye, our family accountant, called me at work and told me Daddy brought my card to the office and showed it to everybody. "Darling, I haven't seen your father that happy in years." I grinned with the thrill of having given my father—and myself—a wonderful gift. After all these years, we had finally connected as father and daughter, if only for a moment.

WILL I BE CRAZY
LIKE YOU?

M Y OLDER SON, AUSTIN, was five, when he asked at breakfast one morning, "Mommy, when I grow up will I be crazy like you?" Zack, three, looked at his brother, then across the table to me. I cringed. When I was a child, I'd wondered the same thing.

I set my hand on Austin's. "No sweetie, you won't be crazy. And neither will you, Zack." I wanted to say there was a difference between *being* crazy and *acting* crazy. And I wanted to believe it. "I'm sorry I scare you boys sometimes," I said. "That's the last thing I want to do."

The incident with Austin occurred shortly after his father moved out. He rented an apartment nearby in Walnut Creek and I kept the big semi-custom house. Even though I'd fought long and hard for my independence, to say it was a difficult time for all of us would be like saying it hurts a wee bit to pull off your fingernails. Compounding the situation was the fact I was still adjusting to the loss of my parents and sorting out all the anger I felt, especially toward my father. Night after night, my parents invaded my dreams. They were unwelcome, gruesome guests who seemed bent on terrorizing me.

My mother had always been the mean one, physically and verbally abusive. She was the most unbalanced, the most neglectful, or so I thought. There were fewer unresolved ill feelings toward her because I'd never expected much from our relationship. But with my father, it was the inverse situation. His shortcomings I'd always managed to overlook, excuse, or diminish. So when he died of heart failure on July 4, 1993, I wasn't relieved but angry and hurt. He didn't tell me he'd been diagnosed with cirrhosis of the liver and he'd allowed himself to die without seeking medical intervention. He hadn't bothered to say good-bye or give me the opportunity. He would never hold my first-born son, who arrived twenty days later.

I cried, as if on cue, when I heard about my father's death. I cried when I saw him lying in the coffin, his smooth, strong hands shriveled and still. I cried when they closed the casket for the final time, when they lowered it into the ground. But between those distinct moments, I was fairly stoic, anesthetized by my shock. When the numbness wore off, when the death finally became real, I realized he wasn't coming back. Then the terrifying dreams began. I started looking back over our relationship and saw that in nearly every aspect, he'd shortchanged me as a father. Grief and Rage stormed the room. That was what, in part, prompted the question, "Mommy, when I'm older, will I be crazy like you?"

A bit of advice: when a careening car comes your way, the safest place might be the sidewalk. I'm embarrassed to admit how much I scared my boys and my ex-husband with my screaming fits. Whenever I felt a sense of injustice I took my rage out on the furniture, my body, the new kitchen cabinets, the pharmacist at Long's. When not consumed with taking care of my boys, I struggled with feelings of anger, betrayal, abandonment and regret. There was an ache I couldn't extinguish.

Once, a teenager sped by me as I pushed my stroller through the neighborhood. I followed her home and wailed at the girl's father the minute he opened the door about how his daughter was unfit for the road. While standing in line at the pharmacy, I lost a screw from my eyeglasses and instead of asking for help, I stood there bawling, tears pouring down my cheeks and shoulders, heaving while everyone tried not to stare.

For months, I wouldn't use the underground parking lot of Walnut Creek's Barnes and Noble after a humiliating crying fit. Suddenly claustrophobic, I had yelled for all the waiting cars to back up and get the hell out of my way so I could get out before I lost my mind. My sons were strapped in their car seats, no doubt scared shitless, wondering why Mommy was going berserk again. I once spent a half-hour washing fresh mushrooms for the risotto, scrubbing off every last bit of dirt, and then threw them into the garbage only to wonder later where they were.

Eventually, my ex-husband agreed to baby-sit the boys as I enrolled in art classes, interior design, graphic design, woodworking, anything to distract me from my grief, to defuse the anger. Then he suggested a writing class. He had no idea how this single activity would save my life.

SCABS
AND SCARS

IN FIRST GRADE, my son Austin was covered limb to limb in scabs. It was his second bout of chicken pox. He and his brother proved that immunizations weren't foolproof. We stood outside his classroom, yet he refused to let go of my arm.

"Please, Austin," I said. "You've already missed a week of school. No one is going to tease you. You're not contagious anymore." Tears puddled in his blue eyes. "Mom really needs to write today. You must stay here."

Until I began writing, my life often felt like a communal toilet overflowing with shit. In conjunction with therapy, writing about my personal struggles helped me to unclog the pipes and flush all the bad stuff away. A ream of paper was the friend I now spent most of my time with on the weekends when my sons were with their father and during weekdays when they were at school. Too much time away from writing and I'd feel acute pangs of withdrawal. In just days, I'd quickly go from happy mom to psycho woman—angry, jittery, talkative—the kind of woman whose instability carries across a room.

I kept promising myself that as soon as I'd purged the last unpleasant memory I'd slow down. But if my son stood beside me scratching his scabs, saying, "Mom, will you play with me now?" there was no way I'd survive till dinner.

I pried Austin's hand from my arm. "You'll be fine," I said. "You'll be fine."

Austin shook his head, scattering tears onto his sweater. Visible through his shiny white hair were the flaking scabs on his scalp. God damn it. Please just do this one thing for me. All I'm asking for is a few undisturbed hours to write. I clenched my fist, wanting so badly to pound it against the wall. Don't cause a scene. Please, Marie. Don't do it.

Austin's science teacher approached. "Excuse me," I said, "could you please help me? I'm trying to get Austin to go inside. He's not contagious anymore but he's embarrassed about the sores."

He studied Austin and frowned. There were even scabs inside my son's ears and by his eyes. "Don't know what you expect me to do. I can't force him."

"But can't you tell him it's okay? I've got so much work to do. I just need some time to write. I, I . . ." I started crying, hung my head, and mumbled, "Please just take him into classroom."

"I'm sorry. I can't help you." He walked away.

Can't or won't? You fucking bastard!

The door opened. Austin's head teacher turned toward us in the hallway. My son and I were having a stare-down, both crying, both refusing to budge. She called to the science teacher. His footsteps stopped.

They huddled for a moment while other tardy parents quickly ushered their children past us. No matter how idiotic I felt, I couldn't stop sobbing.

Austin's head teacher knelt down and said softly, "Austin, do you want to come into class?"

His chest heaved. He shook his head.

"Well, I think another day at home might be good for you. How about if you come back to school tomorrow?"

He nodded. He'd won. They'd all won. I grabbed his wrist and led him away. I'll just sit him on the sofa, I told myself. I'll write, ignoring him until 2 p.m.when it's time to pick up his brother. I'll give him lunch and a snack but I won't play, read, or even talk to him. I'm going to write, God damn it. I need to write. I've played the good nurse, the good mother for a week now. I need to write.

I opened the back door to the Land Rover and said, "Get in and buckle up." I listened for the click of his seat belt then started the endless loop of self-criticism. I hate you, I hate you, you're a despicable mother, you're a cruel person and don't deserve him or his brother. Why'd you have to go and humiliate him? He's just a child. What's one more day out of your fucking life?

And then as usual, the blame shifted to others. But why can't he just do this one thing for me? Why couldn't that stupid man just help me? Who's going to take care of me?

As I was prone to do when everything felt so unjust, frightening, and relentlessly hopeless, I screamed so loudly that anyone standing within fifteen feet of my car, even with the windows rolled up, would have dived head-first into the manzanita hedges. Austin shrieked. We both continued to sob.

I drove home through a blur of tears. Once parked inside

our garage, we stayed in the car another ten minutes, crying. I tried to imagine that the morning had gone differently, that none of this had happened. I was simply sitting at my computer having kissed Austin and Zack good-bye at school like any other day. The hours would go by like minutes. I'd look up and see that I'd written a dozen new pages.

Austin sniffled in the back seat. He wasn't at school. I wasn't at my desk. Our lips and eyelids looked like they'd been injected with collagen.

In the house, Austin slumped on the sofa. I turned on the TV and touched his hand as he scratched at his scabs. "Want me to fix you some chocolate milk?"

When I returned with the milk and a bowl of grapes, he asked, "Will you watch *Home Alone* with me? I'll share my grapes."

What always shamed me the most about these episodes was how forgiving my children seemed afterwards. They'd act extra sweet and clingy as if somehow my tantrum had been their fault. That's the tragedy of the abused child: You think it's your fault. You think you're the shit clogging the drain.

I spread a blanket over our legs. He stared at the television.

GIVE IT
AWAY

I N APRIL 2006, I RENTED a booth at the LA Times Book Festival held on the UCLA campus. My plan wasn't to sell copies of *Storkbites* but to give them away. A cargo van full of them. After an overly-optimistic fourth printing the previous summer, I had eight hundred plus copies of my memoir stacked in our backyard cottage, headquarters of my publishing venture Alluvium Books. Sales had slowed to a trickle, less than a few units a month. Figuring I'd renew some interest in my book, or at the very least, rid our cottage of all those white boxes so my sons could turn the room into a teen hangout, I decided to make the trek to Southern California.

Usually I can talk my friend Lisa or a boyfriend into helping me man a booth for a day or two. But this weekend no one was available. More precisely, no one I cared to be confined with in a 10 x 10 space for roughly twenty hours was available. No one I wanted to give an up-close view of the often humiliating, frustrating side of bookselling. No one who'd resist telling an irritating customer to fuck off.

It takes patience, a sense of humor, and thick skin to respond to some of the comments you hear at a book festival: *Why would anyone be interested in reading or even writing a book like this? How many cookies can we take? Is this another one of those Mommy Dearest books? Do you have any more of those chocolate truffles from last year? What's with all the Mardi Gras posters and beads? You some kind of queen? Have got any lollypops? Got any science fiction? Jesus, our lord and savior, loves you. Know where I can find that book . . . uh . . . don't know the title . . . it's about a kid and he's lost at sea . . . I think with a . . . Marvin, what was it . . . oh, yes, a baboon and a giraffe . . . no, a lion . . . that's it . . . oh, you just sell this book . . . what's it called . . . Storkbites . . . never heard of it . . . Let's go, Shirley, she doesn't have your book . . . Hang on, Marv . . . Where's the closest bathroom?*

In all fairness, I've met many wonderful, warm, intelligent people at these events. To be approached by a reader who says, "I bought your book last year and came back to tell you how much I loved it. Please, keep writing," feels like a genuine hug.

As I prepared for this festival, ordering giveaway pens and chocolates, I remembered someone who'd make a dandy booth partner. Eric, a handsome young mail carrier and striving novelist, lived somewhere in Southern California with his wife and children. In truth, I hardly knew him, met him at a writer's conference in San Diego, cooked dinner for him one night in Walnut Creek when he was in town for a reading. We'd swapped manuscripts, exchanged a half-dozen pleasant, witty e-mails. I figured he was easy-going and might make a suitable partner for the book festival, so I contacted him.

"Bring copies of your novel to sell. You keep the proceeds from your book. I'll pay all the exhibitor's costs in exchange for your help lugging boxes. And if I survive the day, I'll take you out to dinner."

Saturday morning, Eric approached my booth carrying one box of books (versus the twenty-five I'd brought). He gave me a wide, toothy smile, punctuated by two dimples.

"You cut your hair," I said, thinking how he looked less LA-surfer dude and more like good-looking suburban dad. We hugged hello.

"Quite a set-up," he said.

I'd already unwrapped two huge poster boards of enlarged photos of me in full regalia: ball gowns, headpieces, and mantles of sequin, satin, lace, and feathers from my teenage and college Mardi Gras days—Her Majesty Berengaria of Navarre and Her Grace Princess of Tripoli. Behind the folding table, draped in black linens and a floral green fabric to match my book cover, sat suitcases filled with beads, masks, plastic bracelets, and all sorts of trinkets to tie in with the Louisiana theme. Boxes of free chocolate, of course, neon green Frisbees (left over from the 2005 LA Festival), matching gift bags, pens, banners, and all the supplies one needs to set up shop in the middle of a university campus.

Eric pointed to the stack of boxes I'd hired the hotel bellman to help me unload from the rental van. "Planning on selling a shitload of books, eh?"

"I'm giving them away. A last-ditch marketing effort."

His elbow bumped an easel, knocking down Queen Berengaria. After righting the picture, he asked, "This you?"

What kind of woman but one desperate to sell books parades her glory days of Louisiana youth? I felt just as embarrassed now as I did the first time I displayed these photos in the New Orleans airport for a signing. A childhood friend of mine had surprised me, and when he looked at the posters and all the Mardi Gras trinkets I'd displayed, I wanted to crawl under the signing table.

"It's meant to draw people to the booth."

"It'll certainly do that. Can we tell people it's me in drag?"

"Hell. Why not!"

"Put me to work, Queenie."

• • •

BY 9 A.M., ERIC AND I were greeting visitors and offering free copies of *Storkbites*. By ten, he frowned and said, "Who'd ever imagine that giving away books could be so difficult."

People were skeptical. "Free book? What's the catch?" they'd ask and simply step away from the booth, as if we'd made an indecent proposal.

"Some people would rather steal than accept something for free," I said. "Maybe I'll set a box by the stage with a sign: Do not take."

After I sold my condo in San Francisco and packed to move to Walnut Creek, I drove around the Fillmore projects asking every person I saw on the street if they wanted a free, working bike. Each one backed away from my rental truck as if I were one of those perverts their parents had always warned them about. Finally, I parked the truck, took the bike out, and leaned it against a Stop sign near a park. A few minutes later I drove back around, and the bike was gone.

Now one woman who'd stopped by the booth earlier in the morning approached the table a second time. She had been one of those irritating customers who wanted the one color pen we didn't offer. After much deliberation, she settled on another color, and, as if doing us both a favor, took a free copy of *Storkbites* and one of Eric's business cards. I figured she was coming back to complain the pen didn't work.

She placed her copy of my book on the top of the stack and said, "Decided I don't want this." Then without an explanation, she walked off.

"Give back the pen," Eric mumbled and we both giggled.

When he announced that he was going to find a john, I said, "Please don't come back and tell me you saw one of my books in the trash bin. That'd be like finding your love note lying in the gutter."

By early afternoon, we'd only given away a few boxes of books. Doing some rudimentary extrapolation of our give-away rate for the remaining day and a half, I figured if I didn't get a little more proactive, I'd be hauling hundreds of pounds of *Storkbites* back to Walnut Creek. That was not going to happen.

I reminded myself, Rich Shapero, author of *Wild Animus*, had given away tens of thousand of copies of his crappy novel. He went from airport to airport, festival to festival, shoving his books in people's hands.

Eric returned from the bathroom to find a sea of stuffed green bags all around our chairs. I had applied fresh lipstick, combed my hair, checked my nose for bugger flakes. "I'm going to do my Hare Krishna thing," I said. "This could be embarrassing." I grabbed a dozen bags. "So don't watch."

I stood in the middle of the walkway between rows of vendors and made eye contact with people strolling by, smiled, and said, "Would you like a free copy of *Storkbites?* It's a memoir I wrote about growing up in Louisiana." The elevator pitch, simple and quick.

Immediately, my success rate improved. Eric filled bags while I worked the crowds. Many took the bag without looking inside. Some pulled the book out and read the covers to decide if the subject interested them. Others said, "You wrote this? Is this your picture on the cover? Will you sign it?" A few insisted on paying for their copy but then relented. Some wanted to know why I was giving them away, assured me they'd tell their friends, wished me luck. Several read the blurb on the back cover and shared similar experiences. One middle-aged mother with two teen girls told me she'd suffered horrific abuse growing up. The girls rolled their eyes while their mother told me that what helped save her from repeating the cycle with her daughters was the first psychology course she took to become a teacher.

By Sunday mid-afternoon, I was exhausted. The constant smiling. Being in front of people. Crappy festival food. The rejection. The questions. The sad stories shared with me.

Still, as yet another couple approached, I held out a bag and said, "Would you like a copy of my . . ." Before I could finish my pitch, they walked on, eyes averted. I watched them continue on their way, ignoring everyone around them, and wondered, Why come to a book festival if you're not going to buy or look at any books? They stopped at the end of our row of exhibits. The man said something to the woman then turned my way. Embarrassed that he'd caught me watching them, I looked away for a moment then back again. He headed toward me.

"Miss, that was very rude of us just now to ignore you. I apologize. What is it that you've got in those bags?"

"My memoir," I said, feeling my face heat up. "It's called *Storkbites*. I'm giving away free copies to help promote it."

"May I look at one?"

I handed him a book. He studied the picture of the young girl on the cover.

"How old were you here?"

"About four."

"That's sweet." He scanned the back cover, and said, "I'd love a copy. Will you sign it?" After I autographed the book, he patted my arm and wished me much success. I watched him rejoin his wife. She looked in the bag, turned back to me, and smiled.

They continued on their way, and I flashed on situations in which I'd been rude: to telemarketers, absolutely; to greasy guys in Las Vegas who blocked the sidewalks and shoved pornographic cards in my hands, surely; mow and blow guys who come to my front door to solicit business; the mentally challenged bag boy at Whole Foods who always asks how my day is going.

Regardless of what caused this man to turn around and offer up a few minutes of his time, we both, I'm certain, parted feeling like better human beings. Something valuable had been exchanged. Something more than a free book and an apology.

ASKING IS
BEGGING

O NE OF MY FATHER'S MOTTOS was: Never ask! If you have to ask, either you don't deserve it or it's not worth it. Even so, no matter what type of position I held—retailer, waitress, bartender, accountant—throughout high school, college, graduate school, and after, I worked hard and asked for the promotions I deserved. If I didn't get what I wanted, I worked harder or found another job. Often enough, my demands were met and I'd relay the good news to Daddy. He'd cringe and repeat his mantra and I of course would be surprised, yet again, that he hadn't said, "Well done, Sweetheartsabean."

But what does he know? I'd wonder. Others realized my value. He doesn't occupy the cubicle adjacent to mine. He's never had to ask for a raise in his life. Can't it be that sometimes people are so preoccupied they don't realize you've been over-looked? There was nothing wrong with waving your hands and saying, "Hey! Remember me? I'm the one who helped you sign that anchor tenant just when you figured they were headed across the street. I'm the one who always shows up for her Friday night shifts and can cover two stations when we're once again short-staffed. I'm the one who said, 'Give me the bank accounts and I'll find a way to reconcile them.' And in return I'd like some acknowledgement of my contributions—a raise, a promotion, recognition."

My philosophies regarding negotiations were as far apart from Daddy's as Anchorage is from New Delhi—until I encountered The Blonde Bitch. Let's call her B for short. Like my father, B also had a motto: Everyone here is overpaid. You should all just work for free.

When I called to accept her written offer for employment, she cut me off mid-sentence, saying, "Before you go any further, I made a mistake in my letter. The offer is really for thirty-five an hour. Not forty. The forty was my cost including taxes and benefits."

She'd had a weekend to develop a case of buyer's remorse. I should have known better than to accept a job from an employer who prided herself on making a union auditor cry. But since she was the girlfriend of a friend, I decided to give her the benefit of the doubt and said, "Let's split the difference. . . . When do I start?"

I worked for B for two years. She delayed the first salary review for months, rescheduling so many times that I finally left a curt letter on her desk next to a pile of folders marked "Urgent," detailing my contributions to her firm and stating my expectations for fair remuneration. "If we haven't met by Friday," I wrote in closing, "I will assume you're not interested in continuing my employment and you can consider this my two weeks notice."

Until that Friday morning, she completely ignored me. She laughed and chatted with my co-workers in the adjacent offices then walked right past my cubicle. The only contact we had was through my in-box.

At noon on Friday, I looked up from my computer to see her standing there, hands on hips. "Let's meet." I followed her to her office telling myself, Whatever you do, Marie, don't cry. Once seated in her high-back black leather chair, B said coldly, "I was a little shocked by your letter."

I felt my chin start to tremble. She opened a folder with "Marie" scribbled on the tab and handed me a sheet of paper with a bunch of figures, arrows, and bullet points. I half-listened as she ran through the figures—something about eliminating my current benefits like 401K, profit sharing, vacation, and holiday pay, creating a new hourly rate that supposedly factored in all those benefits plus an eleven-percent raise and a Christmas bonus. I paid attention when she said she needed a full-time payroll/accounts receivable accountant. I could continue my part-time employment to be home after school with my sons, but it would be an "at-will" arrangement.

"Let me take this home to look over," I said. There had to be a catch. When her ranch manager had repeatedly asked for a raise, B finally relented. But she also increased the woman's rent so that it more than offset the increase in pay.

On Monday, I accepted her proposal. But at the end of the year, I processed the profit sharing contributions and Christmas bonuses for the employees and realized I hadn't come out ahead. When I expressed my disappointment about my holiday bump, she laughed. "I knew you were going to hit me up for another big raise in January, so I left myself some squiggle room. But I've got an idea. Remember those four hundred dollar Italian boots I bought that you liked? Well, they're too small for me and they should fit you. Do you want them?"

I looked at her as if every blonde joke had been written just for her.

Finally, the absurdity of her offer seemed to register on her face and we both broke out laughing. That was when I knew I was done. There was no point meeting in January to review my salary. I couldn't work for this kind of person any longer. In that moment a plan came together. I'd take out a second mortgage on my house, which had nearly tripled in value since I bought it four years before, and when the loan closed, I'd give my notice. Then I'd work on my next book as I really wanted to.

Around the time I devised this plan, a project manager gave his two weeks notice. B fired him on the spot. Now I knew she might react the same way with me. The day after the loan funded, I told Austin and Zack, "Don't be surprised tomorrow if I come home from work and I've been fired. But it's okay if that happens. Just means I can get started sooner on my writing."

On Monday morning when I dropped Zack off at school, he said, "I hope you get fired today, Mom."

"Thanks, sweetie. Me too."

The first thing I did when I got to work was knock on B's door. "Do you have a few minutes?" If she was going to fire me, I wanted to get it over with so I'd have time to treat myself to a celebratory lunch and maybe do some writing before picking up my boys.

I closed both doors then set the resignation envelope on her desk. To my surprise, she said, "I anticipated this. Will you help me train your replacement?"

Even though I was eager to get out of this environment, I hated to leave my co-workers in a bind. I worked for a couple of months until the new accountant was hired and trained. And for the weeks after my notice period, I charged her seventy-five dollars an hour as an independent contractor.

"Guess you've got me over a barrel," she said, when I threw out the seventy-five dollar figure, the most money I've ever made on an hourly basis. But I had nothing to lose by making a ridiculous request. And we both knew it.

On my last day, I drove from her ranch office, down the windy road that cut through Cull Canyon in Castro Valley, the hills all around were bright green from the winter rain. I thought about my father's motto: If you have to ask, then you don't deserve it. I've since come up with a motto of my own: Don't ask, tell.

THE MOTIVATION
CONUNDRUM

JOHNNY CARSON ONCE QUIPPED, "If life was fair, Elvis would still be alive, and all the impersonators would be dead." Perhaps so. In his fifties, my father was diagnosed with diabetes. When the doctor advised him to quit drinking and smoking, to watch his diet, and to get more exercise, he complained that life was unfair. "What's there to live for? What difference does it make? I'd rather be dead . . ."

"Enough already!" I wanted to scream when Daddy complained yet refused to change his behavior. Giving up smoking and substituting diet for regular cola in his Jack Daniels were his only concessions.

To support him, Momma quit drinking, cold turkey. She didn't point out how suddenly her drinking buddies were otherwise engaged when she invited them to dinner.

For about two weeks after his diagnosis, he abstained from his evening cocktails. But then the occasional highball soon became a half-dozen or more a night. I remember visiting him after he'd resumed drinking at full tilt. He'd nonchalantly get up from his recliner and go to the patio bar. I'd hear the clinking sound of ice falling into a glass, watch him shuffle back into the study with his head hung low, his hand clutching a fresh drink and napkin. Sometimes I'd look over at him, and when he'd meet my gaze, I'd shift my eyes to his drink. He'd say, "I have nothing else to live for." I wanted to slap the pathetic look off his face, shake him and tell him that if I were the one diagnosed with diabetes, he wouldn't catch me wimping out.

Drinking and smoking, for me, were easy addictions to give up once I set my mind to doing so. I saw how the costs far outweighed the benefits. Throughout my teens and twenties I drank so much I had no chance of an intimate relationship. But on January 1st of my 29th year, I quit. Not for health reasons—I was too young to worry about that—I quit to find a husband.

A husband was a means to having children and I desperately wanted kids. There are, of course, less traditional ways of becoming a mother, but I also hoped that, just maybe, in seeking a suitable sperm donor, I might find someone who would cherish me as I would him, someone to complete my dream of house, husband, babies, tennis partner, garden. Guys tended to get a little suspicious when I'd wake up with dragon breath and ask, "Uh, what was your name again? Where did we meet?" And if I hadn't completely scared him off after the first date, then repeating the same anecdotes, asking the same questions—"What do you do for a living? Do you play tennis?"—or telling him the same things over and over—"I just finished my MBA. I'm an accountant. I love to play tennis!"—turned little red flags into neon signs: "Danger, danger . . . step away from the lush."

Smoking, similar motivation. What man wants to look at a red, hacking face, listen to the barking of a seal, and taste rancid nicotine with every kiss?

I should have knocked on wood. Around my 38th birthday, my doctor informed me that I was pre-diabetic and had a fifty-percent chance of developing adult-onset diabetes. The longer I could stave off the disease, the better chance I had of living a long, healthy life. But even fifty-fifty odds sounded rather remote and clinical. I wasn't motivated to alter my diet and lose the extra weight. At this point in my post-divorce life, I wasn't interested in dating, so being naked in front of a man wasn't an issue.

One stern warning after another, plus outsized scores on my glucose tests, made me see that I was slowly killing myself. As much as I hated to admit it, I had begun to whine just like my father. "What kind of life will this be if I can only eat meat, beans, and vegetables? Gone are smoothies, cranberry juice, ice cream, pizza. This is so unfair?"

For two years, I went on and off a rigid diet. Whenever I felt depressed or pissed off at the world, little comforted me like Godiva chocolates or a bear claw oozing with brown sugar. Some people, when unhappy, turn to alcohol, cigarettes, or some other addiction like extreme exercise or sex. Healthier people might look to friends or support groups or meditation. But my preferred drug was now sugar.

Whenever I'd slip and dope up on the forbidden sweets, I'd hate myself for not considering my boys reason enough to lead a healthier lifestyle. For months at a time, I'd get perverse and eat whatever I wanted. I didn't care if I was constantly peeing, high on cake one minute, down from withdrawal the next.

One Friday evening, I was soaking in a steaming bath after a two-hour springboard dive workout. The pool's chlorine had made my feet itchy. I grabbed my foot and started scratching around my painted red toenails. The more I scratched, the worse the itch burned. Turning my feet over, I separated my toes to inspect. Between each digit, the skin had peeled away, leaving pink, cracked flesh. What the hell is going on? I looked at my other foot. More sores, some deeper. This can't be good.

I'd been monitoring this athlete's foot problem for weeks, dousing myself with antifungal. But with all the swimming, softball, hiking, and tennis, the cracking and peeling had now spread to the balls of my feet. Would my legs be next? I remembered a newspaper article I'd read on diabetes about the number it did on feet. The author said that because the disease could lead to reduced circulation, sores often took longer to heal. Proper shoes, socks, and skin maintenance were essential to avoiding serious complications that could lead to amputation.

Staring at my scaly toes, I thought about our former housekeeper, Juanita, who had attended Daddy's funeral. Still so pretty despite the wrinkles and gray hair, she walked slowly up to my sisters and me to express her condolences. When I asked how she was, she said, "Good. I'm still working for that nice family. Had some feet problems. Diabetes. Doctors took my toes. But I thank God everyday I can still walk."

I was shocked by her accepting attitude.

"You just take what life deals out," she said. "Make the best of it."

Yeah, I thought now as I sat in the tub, or you can whine—why me, why me, why me for fuck's sake!

Then it hit me. How I would dive without toes? Or feet? Or legs? There was no way I could balance on the board on two stubs. I thought of how excited and proud I felt each time I successfully completed a new dive. Softball, hiking, even tennis I could give up if I had to, but diving I hoped would see me into my twilight years.

It is embarrassing to admit that the image of me standing with peg legs on a diving board was what moved me from the remoteness of concern to the intimacy of motivation. My love of a sport—not my boys (though I love them dearly), not my own well-being—was the catalyst I needed to take my health seriously.

CAN WE DO
IT AGAIN?

SITTING IN A SMOKE-FILLED corner of the Hotel Pierre Bar in New York, I leaned over a dish of tiny pickled green tomatoes and exclaimed, "Well, listen to this one . . ."

The five men in our party, having just run the New York Marathon, puffed away on their celebratory cigars and smiled along with the women as we sat around a small table. We were trading how-stupid-was-this? stories of our misadventures as parents.

"In 2000, my boys and I rented a house in Walnut Creek that sat at the top of a steep hill," I said, telling them how every morning, with my sons strapped in their seats, I'd stop my Honda CRV near the bottom of the long driveway and pick up my newspaper. A few times, when I was in a hurry, I'd simply press on the brake, unhitch my seat belt, open the door, and reach down. But one day when I leaned out and over, straining to grab the yellow plastic bag, my sandal slipped. The car lurched forward. In an instant I was falling out onto the asphalt. I hit the ground and spun around to reach for my door handle, but the back tires of the car rolled right past me.

"Someone, help!" I shouted. The car picked up speed, crossed one of Walnut Creek's busiest streets, and headed straight toward a cable fence.

Listening to my story, everyone but my neighbor Glenn gasped. Much to my humiliation, he knew about the whole mess all too well. I'd transferred my insurance over to his agency shortly before the accident.

I explained how I jumped up and ran after the boys, praying for the car to stop when it hit the fence. Instead, it ripped through the cable, clipped branches from two narrow trees, and then raged downward through the brush. I yelled for my neighbors to call 911 and got that sick feeling I had when I lost the boys in a department store.

Here, I paused, reflecting on how guilty I'd felt chasing after my boys, knowing they might die if the CRV rolled over and caught fire. At the time, it seemed like divine retribution. I had screamed at them when I'd opened the garage and found their action figures strewn about the driveway. We were late for swim practice again. I yelled and stomped my feet, warning that if they couldn't take care of their toys, I'd throw them away. Then I climbed into the car, slammed the door so hard that my iced tea in the cup holder fell and splashed all over my sandals. It was probably the wet brakes that caused my foot to slip. Now I wondered if God was going to take away my sons to punish me for being so careless, so mean.

Following the car, I imagined the terror in my boys' bright blue eyes. I thought of those parents like Susan Smith who sent her car into a lake to drown her children. Would people wonder if I had done this on purpose? Please, God, I begged. Don't take my boys away from me. I'll be a better mother. I swear.

"Austin, Zack," I called after them. "I'm so sorry. Mommy loves you both so much."

The car roared on through my neighbor's side yard. Near the bottom of the hill sat a parked truck. Oh, shit . . . thankfully the Honda missed the truck and veered off to the left, heading toward an old boat. Somehow it missed the boat then lurched for a wooden fence. Finally, after bulldozing an entire section of fence, the car thumped to a halt.

I reached the car and yanked open the back door praying I wouldn't find two bloodied, banged-up boys. I leaned in and found the boys sitting there with total blank stares. They weren't even crying. Zack's eyes had fully dilated. Austin's unreadable face changed to a sneer. It said that I had really fucked up.

We sat on the bumper of the nearby old truck, my legs bleeding from the first fall and from the subsequent tumble down the hillside. I sobbed and tried to tell the neighbor who came out with her cell phone, apparently talking to a 911 dispatcher, that we were OK.

Months later, safe at the bar with my friends, I could still hear the roaring sirens. An ambulance, two police cars, a fire engine all arrived as I hugged my boys and told them over and over how sorry I was.

Zack, in his sweet five-year-old voice, said, "Mommy, what happened? I went to sleep right after you opened your door and fell out." He giggled. His dilated eyes blinked rapidly from his state of shock. "Can we do it again? It was fun!"

Austin elbowed his little brother and stared at me before looking down at my grass-stained, bleeding legs. I had lost my sandals somewhere along the chase. He didn't find the episode funny. I sobbed harder. For a week following the accident he wouldn't ride with me on highways or in heavily trafficked areas.

We gave our story to several police officers and declined a ride in the ambulance. The officers congratulated my boys for having fastened their seat belts and gave them silver badge stickers. They seemed as amazed as I was that they'd crossed one of the busiest roads in town without hitting another car.

The tow truck guys shook their heads, trying to figure out how my car had managed to steer itself along the windy course and how they'd be able to pull it to the road without removing the nearby trees. One female officer, after asking me such questions as "Who is the president?" and "What month is it?" told me I was her second fall-out-of-the-car call that week.

"I do stupid stuff like that all the time," said one of my marathon-running friends in the hotel bar. "I'm always in a rush to grab the paper and skim the financial pages."

His wife swallowed. Was she thinking about their newborn baby strapped into a runaway car? "Well, you'd better stop doing that."

PLAYING
FAVORITES

I WAS SITTING IN A SWANKY living room of a Victorian flat on Sacramento Street in San Francisco. Across the way in the well-manicured park, gay men frolicked in the bushes. In this same quaint neighborhood, men and women with pockets of balled-up Safeway bags nodded hello to each other as their well-groomed dogs took a dump on the dewy lawn. As for me, I was waiting for the well-put-together woman seated next to me on the sofa to review her notes on my twenty-page manuscript. My black jeans, black sweater, and black clogs looked as out of place in this airy, crème-colored, well-appointed room as a cargo ship docked in a field of wheat.

Up to now, this lady was simply a curt voice on the telephone, a photograph on a flyer offering private writing classes and consultation. "Let's start here," she said. "I want to better understand the relationship of these sisters. These children to their parents."

I looked at the page she held on the lap of her beige slacks and shrugged. "What exactly do you want to know?"

"We've got all your sisters and their families in a room. Dad's now dead. His chair is noticeably empty. Your mother is off in her bedroom hacking away, possibly dying, and you are all just carrying on as if it's Christmas as usual. What are the relationships among you? Which sister aligns with which other sister? Who do you, Marie, avoid sitting next to? Avoid talking to? With whom do you exchange a glance when something is said that you don't agree with? Pan the room as if you've got a camera in your hands. Let us see the interactions. I want to know each sibling's role in the family. For instance," she said, mentioning one of my older sisters. It took me a second to mentally cross-reference the pseudonym with the actual since I'd only recently changed the names to appease my family. "Seems to me she's the blackest of the black sheep."

"That sums it up," I said and felt a stab of anger toward my mother for the way she terrorized my sister with brutal beatings and name-calling.

"Blackest of the black sheep," she repeated, fairly pleased with herself. "I like that. You can have it if you'd like. It's my gift to you."

My gift to you. Fuck that "gift shit," lady. I'm paying you five hundred dollars to read a twenty-page excerpt and to give me one hour of your time.

She was silent. My eyes followed hers to the lined tablet I was holding.

"Oh, yes. Let me write that down before I forget," I said then scribbled "blackest of the black sheep." I saw in my mind a pasture with three well-fed, well-groomed white-and-woolies lazing about under the shade of a massive oak. A hundred yards away, set apart from the others, there were six black sheep, mere specks on the horizon, huddled nose to nose, seeking refuge in the narrow shadow of a scrawny shrub. In the middle of the black dots stood the charcoal queen: malnourished and dejected, yet defiant.

We started on page one of an excerpt from *Storkbites* and went through her comments. I took copious notes, asking for clarification or suggestions, which I would take home and mull over before either incorporating into the manuscript or ignoring altogether. It felt as if only ten minutes had passed when she stood to signal that my hour was up. "You've got a lot of good material here," she said, handing me the pages now bearing both our scribbles. "Material that some writers would kill for."

I smiled awkwardly, wondering, Is my family legacy really something to be proud of? To be envied?

We shook hands, and as she opened the front door for me, I thought how that was probably the fastest five hundred dollars I'd ever blown. Digging my car keys from my jean pockets, I spotted a man in a suit emerging from the thicket at the far end of the park. He glanced around then quickly brushed off his dark slacks. I frowned. Not at the man. I didn't care what any guy did in the bushes as long as it was consensual and private, relatively speaking, that is. What made me frown was that I'd just spent five hundred dollars on top of another ten thousand (paid to a different editor) and I still didn't have a happy ending, a clear-cut path through my story. "Dig deeper." That's all I ever heard. How much deeper was I supposed to go?

As I headed to the Bay Bridge, I mumbled above the song on the radio. Blackest of the black sheep. Wasn't it enough to be the black sheep of the family? But the blackest of the black? How could my parents have treated one of their own children so darkly? I could see my sister in all her timidity, the pain of her life etched in her darting eyes, and I was furious, so furious even now that I wanted to ram the driver ahead of me who'd changed into my lane and caused me to swerve out of his way.

My siblings and I all vied for my father's affection. Some of us in vain. I've always wondered, out of nine children, or even just two, how does a parent decide to favor one over another? Is it a conscious choice? Do you hold your newborn in your arms and feel something different about this baby than you did with the three that came before or the five that came after?

My father claimed that he strived for fairness. Maybe he did. But the disparities were clear to those of us in the black sheep category.

When my mother came to our rooms to deliver a beating, he ignored our cries for help if we weren't his favorites. When she announced a new house rule at the dinner table that applied only to the blackest of the black, Daddy didn't say a word. I remember countless times walking into his study and being greeted warmly, but later I watched his face really light up when another sister entered the room. He'd bring his recliner to a full upright position and plant his feet firmly on the olive-green carpet as she approached with a kiss. He'd mute the TV and say, "Hi, darling. Won't you sit?"

Try to tell me these differences don't matter. That they don't pit one sibling against the other. Or wall off the haves from the have nots. The upshot is a sense of deprivation that may take an entire lifetime to fill.

Now, fourteen years after my parents' deaths, I find myself less judgmental. Time has afforded me greater perspective and compassion. No matter how I try not to, sometimes I feel differently about my boys. This is something I would have never imagined as I held each one in my arms at the moment of birth. I love each of my sons so very much and try to treat each equally. But at various stages of their lives, our personalities have either meshed or not. Our interests and dispositions have converged or not. Austin or Zack might go through a period of acting out an air of entitlement, which would then make me want to humble him by giving less.

My way of playing favorites has nothing to do with preference, choosing or avoiding one child over the other, or with playing the games my parents played. My goal isn't to bruise. It may be simply that Austin's needs *are* more urgent in the moment, and his demands feel so overwhelming that I have little time or energy left for Zack. When Zack is willing and able to be more independent and allow his brother to dominate my attention for a while, I've allowed it. Then I feel guilty. And sometimes it's just easier to sit on the bed drawing cartoons with Zack than to play pickleball in the driveway with Austin, my more competitive son.

I used to think my father favored the children who were most like him. But in looking back now, it seems he was drawn to those who displayed both confidence and compliance. Perhaps he found it too painful to accept those of us who displayed certain weaknesses he didn't want to see in himself. Maybe he was drawn to the children who mirrored the man he wanted to be. Certainly he didn't aspire to be the blackest of black.

I mirrored my father in art, and to a lesser degree, in my aptitude for business. These were our two points of convergence. Otherwise, I felt like a cat in his dog-eat-dog world. I reflected back a Ma-ree he didn't want to see—a messy, impertinent, willful, questioning, independent person.

With my boys I try to see them not as reflections of myself but as unique individuals. Sometimes they'll analyze a situation with such clarity and maturity, which I don't even possess, and I'm dumbfounded. I can't believe how confident they are. Their convictions might be opposite to mine but I like that they are willing to be who they are and feel assured of my love despite our differences.

Had my father lived past his sixty-five years, hung on in his study for another decade until I'd grown into a seasoned parent, I might have come to accept him more while he was still alive. I might have viewed him not from a place of deprivation or abandonment, nor put him on a lofty pedestal. I could have seen him for who he was, who he was not, and who I wanted him to be.

THE FAMILY
CODE

"DON'T TELL THEM DADDY'S DEAD," one of my sisters fussed after I'd hung up on another telemarketer. About every third call to my parents' house was from someone who sounded as if he were calling from twenty leagues under the sea (or India) to sell one investment, subscription, long distance plan, or Bombay vacation timeshare to whatever name popped up on his computer screen.

"Say he's not available," she said and lit a cigarette. "We don't want *them* to know Momma is here alone. Haven't you heard stories about widowers cheated out of their money?"

She was right, I suppose. For all you know, Ravi Telemarketer could be a murderer or a rapist. Certainly I didn't want to see a photo of my mother on the front page of *The Daily Advertiser*: "Local Widow Found Slain: Daughter didn't heed her sister's advice!" But I also hated the idea of Momma being constantly reminded that Daddy, her husband of fifty years, was dead and that she was now alone.

In defiance of my sisters, I continued to tell the submerged voices on the other end of the line that, "No, Mr. Etienne won't be renewing his subscription to Playboy or Forbes as he is dead. He won't be doing much reading from the great beyond."

Sometimes with family and friends you have to agree to disagree. So this was what we did. After the funeral, and later when in town visiting, I responded to the solicitous phone calls with my usual sarcasm and honesty, while my sisters, those who didn't simply let the answering machine see the callers to the door, were polite yet evasive. This problem, as it turned out, was short-lived.

Six months after Daddy's death, my mother was taken from her bedroom by ambulance. Her steady diet of vodka and prescription pills landed her in the ICU at Our Lady of Lourdes. Four months after being admitted to the hospital, Momma died and we disconnected her phone.

• • •

I GREW UP ENGULFED IN SUCH FEAR that as an adult I don't know which is more frightening: suffocating from fear or facing it. Buried up to my nose in sand—one bucketful after another of "You can't do this . . . Don't say that . . . Oh, no, what if . . . Don't believe what you see . . ."—at times I've found myself so firmly rooted in a pit of terror I feared I'd never escape. Now I'm more like a dog: the harder you try to yank the stick from my mouth, the harder I'll clamp down.

Tell me I'll suffer heat stroke if I go to Ixtapa, Mexico, in the middle of August and that's exactly when I'll book my next vacation. Movie starts in ten minutes and you say there's no way we can drive across town, find a parking spot, and buy tickets and popcorn. Just watch me. Claim the company's bank records are beyond reconciliation. With a quiet office, a fast computer, and a supply of Diet Coke, I'll prove you wrong.

As January 1, 2000 approached, Y2K, people all over the world were holding their collective breath, except in remote areas like Kenya and Somalia where famine and drought typically take precedence over whether you'll be able to access your ATM or get a blended Frappaccino before your caffeine headache kicks in. At the stroke of midnight, our technologically-obsessed civilization would suddenly turn into a huge pumpkin. So commentators around the globe said the time was running short to stock up on gasoline, drinking water, firewood, peppermint Schnapps, condoms, and KY Jelly (for those dark, cold nights when you and your partners or cousins tire of charades).

Unable to accept the whole doomsday notion, I rented a condo at Lake Tahoe and spent the week leading up to Y2K with my boys, making snowmen, skiing, drinking hot chocolate, and glancing through magazines like Cosmopolitan— "Ladies: Your horoscope for 2000! Romance. Success. Weight Loss." (Unless, of course, we all die in a mass riot.)

On New Year's Eve, I sat with my sons on a worn sofa, which based on its appearance and odor, was from the same era as the rental's red shag carpet, and flipped back and forth between channels, from the hoopla in Times Square to familiar cartoon reruns. Each of us took turns watching what we wanted for a few minutes. At the stroke of midnight, I grabbed control of the remote. When the ball dropped, I checked my watch. Twelve o'clock. Dick Clark, in all his preserved youthfulness, hadn't been zapped off the screen or the planet. And the florescent light in the kitchen was still humming. We weren't going to die. I smiled, more relieved than I'd expected.

"We're still here," I said to my boys, kissing each of them, then tearing open a party-size bag of fortune cookies.

"Of course, we are," Austin said, so matter-of-fact. There was little talk of Y2K on Nickelodeon or in second grade math.

Zack reached over and cracked open a fortune. "Read it."

While I can't remember exactly what this particular piece of paper said, I clearly recall being disappointed once I realized there were only seven different sayings in the whole lot. One cookie after another, the fortunes repeated themselves. However, I would like to think Zack's cookie said something like this: "Those who fear life are already half dead."

• • •

T HE NEXT DAY WE SLEPT until mid-morning. I could almost taste the blinding white rays of the sun in the crisp mountain air. Icicles hanging from the roof dripped like iridescent popsicles.

The boys watched cartoons and ate Captain Crunch while I packed the car. The only precautions I had taken in the unlikely event of Y2K calamity was to fill up my gas tank so I could make it back home, buy two gallons of spring water, and withdraw one thousand dollars from my bank account. What a relief to be able to waste one of the water containers de-icing my windshield.

Once we were buckled up, I turned on the radio, hitting the seek button every couple of seconds to find a station that would satisfy the three of us. It was reassuring to know everyone was broadcasting. Somewhere on this first day of January 2000, I was certain, John Wayne was filling a TV screen with American machismo. And in other parts of our perfect world, for the introductory price of $49.50, you could order on QVC your very own crystal enchantress ring. And for only $14.99, you could get the matching pendant!

That afternoon, I called one of my sisters to wish her a happy New Year. After we exchanged greetings, she said, "I have some bad news. It's not any of the sisters," she quickly added so I wouldn't panic. "Aunt Jean died. Apparently murdered."

Murdered? I thought of my brother Chess and cringed.

"She was found sitting at her dining room table. She'd been working on her taxes."

"Her taxes? It's only January first."

"A neighbor hadn't seen her outside in a couple of days so he called her son. There was blood everywhere. There's going to be an investigation."

"How awful. Why would someone want to kill her?"

"Rumor around town is she took a lot of money out of the bank and even sold her stocks to buy more gold coins. Fear of Y2K. I don't know if you know this, but she had a rather large coin collection, hidden all over the house." I pictured the giant in the tale of "Jack and the Bean Stalk" sitting at his table in the clouds, bludgeoned to death, his gold coins whisked away in the rush of night.

"At one of the family dinners a while back," my sister said, "she asked me if I wanted to see some of her quilts. Do you know a week ago she showed up with two huge Glad bags crammed full of quilts? They were unbelievably gorgeous. One looked like stained glass. She kept saying how she loved making them and couldn't wait to start the next one."

"Was there a necktie one in the bunch?" Momma had given her sister Daddy's expensive ties after his death to make a patchwork quilt. Maybe we could ask her son for that one back.

"Not that I recall. Why?"

"Nothing." Our poor cousin. First his dad dies and now his mother. No brothers or sisters. "Not a very positive start to the new millennium," I said. "I think I might go out and buy a pork roast, some cabbage, and black-eyed peas, for good luck." This was the New Year's Day meal my mother had always prepared. Each item held some significance I couldn't exactly remember other than in total the meal was supposed to ward off misfortune. "We all might need it."

When I hung up, I recalled the last time I'd seen my aunt, a heavy-set, strong-willed woman. It was in Opelousas at a family Christmas dinner. She told me about a recent trip to Europe she'd gone on after her husband's death three years earlier. She wasn't going to be the sort of widower to sit around her house and mope.

A couple of days later my sister called me again. "The obit says Aunt Jean died of multiple wounds. At first the cops treated it like an accidental death. Can you believe that? How does someone accidentally spray blood all over herself and her kitchen table without even leaving behind a bloody weapon? When they performed the autopsy, they found her throat had also been cut. From the sound of it, she put up one hell of a fight." That last detail I could have done without. To think that she fought for her life, that she knew what was happening.

In the days that followed I phoned my younger sister, a Lafayette cop, who spoke to one of the officers at the scene.

She said there was no visible sign of entry, figured the murderer might have been someone our aunt knew: a bank clerk, a pal from the coin shop, a friend she'd confided in, or someone even closer. The officers had botched the investigation, trampling all over the crime scene, failing to read key suspects their rights. No arrests were ever made, just like with Chess's death. The gold was never found. After the house was sold, my cousin moved away. Who knows what happened to all those beautiful quilts.

• • •

F EAR HAS A WAY OF TIPTOEING back into your life uninvited. Since my Aunt's death, I've found that I'm now most comfortable off the radar. My two sons and I live in a modest house in Northern California after having sold the fancy two-story home my ex-husband and I bought shortly before our separation. When we first moved into our three-bedroom, two-bath rancher, my younger son invited a friend over from school. As I pulled into the driveway, he said with a shy voice, "I'm sorry we don't have carpets. We only have wooden floors."

Later at dinner, after his friend had gone home, I told both boys they didn't need to be ashamed of our house. "It's not that we can't afford carpeting," I added, gently. "Many people actually prefer hardwood floors. And often it's even more expensive."

Maybe it's being kids of a divorce, a minority in a fairly affluent area with a seemingly greater than average number of intact families, or maybe my frightening tirades when the boys were younger imprinted them with insecurities. They complain regularly that we have the lamest car, a '99 Honda CRV that struggles to make it up the mountains to Lake Tahoe. I tell them a cheap, dependable car suits our needs perfectly and reduces my frustration at having to deal with service centers. "If it makes you feel better," I say, "I'll by a Mercedes hood ornament and hot glue it to the hood." They roll their eyes. I just don't get it.

But I do. And to be honest, fear plays a role in why we live in a modest house and don't own a luxury car. Partly, I don't want to attract the envy of others. I don't want to flaunt something that might give others reason to set aside their conscience and cause our family harm. I don't want to be sitting at my table one New Year's Eve and find my throat slashed and my riches stolen.

Fourteen years have passed since my father's death, since the time I stubbornly refused to say, "Mr. Etienne is not available. Please call back at another time." I now have two sons, and I am divorced and on my own. What do I tell my boys when I leave them alone? I'm sure it's what every other mother tells her child: "If anyone you don't know calls, don't tell them I'm not here." I've realized that in this way, I guess I'm just one of the family.

IT'S MY
PARTY

IN ONE OF MY OLD FAMILY ALBUMS, there is a picture of me on my fifth birthday. Poised on the edge of a red velvet living room chair, I'm wearing a plaid party dress, and I'm surrounded by a brand new hula-hoop and an abundance of gifts. The smile on my face is genuine. It says I'm special. We're celebrating *me* today. Take the photo fast so I can open my presents.

As birthdays approached, my siblings and I would write out a list of all the toys we wanted and my parents would produce these items (within reason—we never got a pet monkey) along with cake, candles, and song. But after more than a decade of doing this for each of their nine children (almost a birthday a month) they tired of the ritual. In lieu of presents, they would now buy a card, tuck a generous check inside, and sometimes prepare a favorite meal or take us out to dinner.

By the time I entered college, my parents tended to forget our birthdays altogether. Sometimes in the evening they'd call, drunk, just before bedtime, and say, "Happy birthday, darling. Stop by tomorrow to pick up your check." It was hurtful to be overlooked by my own parents. My siblings and I eventually began reminding our parents of each other's birthdays. So if my mother called at noon with birthday wishes and a sudden invite for dinner, I'd feel certain some little fairy sister had whispered in her ear. I'd phone the usual suspects until prying loose a confession, as they'd do with me. Why did we need to confirm that once again we'd been nearly forgotten? I suppose to reinforce our belief that we were not special enough to be remembered.

When my 40th birthday approached, I could feel sadness creeping up on me as it tends to do now every May. Fearing that none of my friends or family would get around to throwing me a party to celebrate this milestone, I decided to preempt them. I sent out invites for a swimming party. Immediately, some of my closest friends began to hem and haw about whether or not they'd attend.

One said, "That's right in the middle of little Johnny's nap time." Others responded with maybes, like "If nothing else comes up," or "If I drop five pounds before then so I don't humiliate myself in a swimsuit."

One friend accused me of thoughtlessly choosing a Saturday when I knew her husband's only day off was Sunday. She added that her two older children, now pre-teens, refused to be dragged to their mom's friend's party, and the younger children (still in diapers and not yet swimmers) would need a sitter and they were all booked up. Feeling sorry for myself, I sent her an e-mail, saying, "I'm tired of being taken for granted, tired of begging you to treat me as if our friendship matters." I received no response. No card, no gift, no offer such as, "Since I can't make the party, how about I take you to lunch next week." Nothing like a bunch of wussies to make one feel special. Or maybe . . . they were begging off because they'd planned a surprise party.

A woman I'd just begun cultivating a friendship with replied with a resounding yes. Apparently she hadn't received word of the surprise."What can I bring?" she asked. "Do you need some help? Don't worry about my kids, they'll come whether they want to or not."

The morning of the party, I worked in my kitchen, preparing guacamole and slicing fruit while feeling resentful, then sorry for myself, then ashamed for feeling resentful and sorry for myself. After all, my moaning would've been all for naught if my friends really did show up.

By the time I left my house for the pool, I couldn't wait to be done with the day. I was exhausted from my self-defeating thoughts, needing my so-called friends' approval to feel that I wasn't worthless. I set myself up for disappointment: No matter how the party went, it wouldn't be good enough to make me feel loved.

Besides the lifeguard and my dive coach, who was working on small projects around the facility and hugged me hello, my sons and I were the first to arrive. No one jumped out from behind the bleachers or the equipment shed or the oleanders. They weren't hiding in the boys' and girls' bathrooms listening for a call from the lookout person. But those who did show up, those who did make the effort, I'll always remember.

My second celebration, a complete success, came a month later in the form of a six-day river rafting trip in the Grand Canyon. Here on the river no one knew I had just turned forty. I was simply a single woman on an adventure with a group of likeminded thrill-seekers: riding the mighty rapids of the Colorado River and exploring caves by day, and at night, sharing meals and stories, bathing in the cold blue water, and sleeping on the shores.

From the Grand Canyon, the festivities continued. I caught a propeller plane to Las Vegas where I'd made reservations at the Bellagio for three days of indulgence: deep-tissue massages, Cirque du Soleil's "O" water show, shopping, movies in bed, and unhurried meals with a novel in hand. Not once did I feel lonely or consider myself unloved. Turns out, I'm damn good company. And I'll always remember my birthday.

HANDYMAN'S
ASSISTANT

M Y HANDYMAN MARK, a part-time actor and tap dancer, had done minor home repairs for me for nearly eight years, and we'd gotten to be friends. My boys liked him because he could magically turn a red electrical wire into licorice. I liked him because he wasn't creepy to have around like so many of the men who rang my door bell and said, "You called for a plumber?" or "I'm here to install new locks on your doors." I'd watch Mark work, follow him from his truck to my house and back to his truck, getting the latest update on his dating adventures and new business ideas. He'd ask about my writing and diving, how the boys were handling the divorce. Mark desperately wanted to be a father, so I shared silly parenting anecdotes.

One day he came over to tackle a list of projects I'd set aside for him. He mentioned that his business was growing and he needed an assistant. The timing couldn't have been better for me. It was the new millennium and the Internet bubble had burst. My tech stocks, a large percentage of the portfolio I'd inherited from my parents, had lost nearly half their value. I needed extra income and yet hated the idea of returning to accounting. On impulse, I suggested that I be his new assistant.

He hesitated for a moment, probably thinking, She hires me to change batteries in her smoke detectors and switch out her toilet seats. How much help can she offer me? But finally he agreed to give it a shot.

The first house we approached was in a gated community. Mark whispered, "The husband just moved out." I nodded and wondered if five years ago he had mentioned this fact about me to one of his former assistants. A petite woman answered the door. Two young girls padded across the floor and clung to their mother's legs as Mark introduced me. I pictured myself from her vantage: a youngish, blonde-haired woman, not so unlike herself, dressed more for tennis than ladders and power tools. I shook her hand, enjoying her curious smile, and wondered how many more Christmases this downsized family would spend here.

As the holidays approached, Mark's clients had endless lists of projects they wanted completed before family and friends arrived. So he took on my dive coach, Steve, as a second assistant. In winter, Steve's swim school closed down except for diving and he often helped me with painting projects around my house.

The day before our first job as a threesome, I bought some "easy to install" book shelves for my own bedroom. Since I was now a handyman's assistant, the least I could do was practice on my own projects. I read the instructions carefully, something I rarely did when I sewed or bought new appliances, and began fitting the wooden pieces together. But every time one side aligned, the other would pop out of the grooves. Quickly, my frustration grew. With each attempt, I made a little more progress. But then an edge would refuse to align and the whole unit would go off kilter. It felt like the bookshelf was mocking me: "Handyman's assistant, ha!"

After another futile hour, I lost it. What does *lost it* look like? Picture a woman with clenched fists, shrieking at top volume with the windows open, "Come on, you stupid fucker! Fit! Why won't you fit, God damn it?" Picture a woman grabbing piece after piece of shelving, striking the floor so hard the wood turns to kindling, then sobbing red-faced on the splinters. When I finally quit crying and my heart stopped pounding, I gathered all the broken pieces, the unused screws and hardware, the packing material, and the inane instructions, and shoved them into the outside garbage so my boys wouldn't ask any questions.

The following morning our little work crew met at a job site in Blackhawk, a gated community in which many professional Bay Area athletes live. Mark pointed to a stack of white boxes and said, "You two assemble these shelves for the garage while I start on the lighting in the house." He opened the back door to the house and just before he left us alone, he said, "Holler if you need help." Like yesterday? I thought.

"It might be easier if we work together, one unit at a time," I suggested. Steve agreed and we opened the first box carefully so we wouldn't lose any of the screws. Turned out this unit didn't come with screws.

"Have you ever put one of these together?" Steve asked. There was hesitancy in his voice.

"Never. I'm happy to defer to your expertise."

"Thanks a lot."

He studied the instruction booklet while I read over his shoulder. Steve knew the ins and outs of maintaining three pools and a solar heating system, staffing and running a swim center, coaching dive students, but he was new to this handyman business as well.

"Looks like we attach the long pieces to the side and back brackets," I said. "These thingamajigs slip into the corresponding holes. The wooden shelves go in last."

We matched the male and female parts together until we had a wobbly, standing skeleton of a shelving unit. Simultaneously, we both let go to grab another bracket and the thing fell over, metal clanging on the concrete.

"Crap," I said, just as Mark reentered the garage.

"How's it going?"

Steve and I looked up. "Oh fine," I said. "We're sort of figuring it out as we go."

We watched Mark grab some tools from his truck. After he'd gone back inside the house, Steve said, "How about you hold it together while I fit the pieces on?"

Using my knees, calves, arms, and hands as braces, I kept the scaffold upright while Steve tapped the brackets into place. Once the frame was hooked together, he began slipping in the shelves. When he tried to squeeze the last plank into the bottom space, there wasn't enough room.

"Oh, well," he said, not seeming the least bit frazzled. "We'll try it in reverse order." This would have been a useful suggestion to include in the instruction manual, but "we" managed to figure it out on our own.

"Perfecto! We did it," he said. We exchanged high fives the same way we did when I'd mastered a scary new dive.

"Not so difficult when you've got an extra pair of hands," I said, more to myself than to Steve. It felt like such a huge accomplishment. I hadn't gone ape-shit.

With each successive unit, we gained more confidence. It was fun working shoulder to shoulder, finagling the more stubborn pieces until they locked together. I imagined this was what it would be like to work as brother and sister, one of the many things I missed out on after losing my brothers.

By noon, the shelving units were lined up along the empty far wall of the garage. The owner came outside to inspect our work. He smiled and said, "Good job."

I worked part-time for Mark for several months until it became clear he needed a full-time assistant. One of the greatest pleasures of this job, besides snooping inside the lives of the super wealthy—professional athletes, CEO's, old money— was seeing how pleased the clients were by even the smallest improvements to their homes. I learned a lot by watching Mark troubleshoot a situation when things didn't go according to plan. He was grumpy at times, complained under his breath, like when we were hired to install a gate on a redwood fence and it refused to align properly. But instead of taking a sledge hammer and knocking down the entire fence, like I might have done if it were mine, he simply improvised. This taught me everything in life doesn't have to be perfect. It just needs to function. Sometimes the smallest change makes things better.

FORGIVENESS

DURING THE DECADE SINCE MY parents' deaths (and after the settlement of their estates), I broke off all contact with one of my sisters. Anger, hurt, and a feeling of superiority festered in me until I'd said some harsh words I couldn't take back. Even though I missed her at times, inquired about her, felt sad that she'd never met my youngest son who closely remembered her in appearance, I was too stubborn, too pissed to make amends. In the early years after our falling out, friends suggested that I forgive her. But I couldn't. Later, when I felt almost ready, I was afraid she'd reject me.

In all the years we didn't speak, not one of her birthdays went by without me sitting here in California wondering what she was doing in Louisiana. Was she having a good day? Had her friends remembered her? Or was she sad, home alone, feeling unloved? Times when we were close, I'd phone her on her birthday, hear the sorrow in her voice, and wish I could make it all better.

In the last few years of our estrangement, I worried my sisters might forget her birthday. I'd call around, casually remind them, and ask if they were taking her to dinner or inviting her out for some fun.

In 2003, when *Storkbites* appeared in bookstores around our hometown, it seemed our fate would be permanently sealed: We'd never speak or see each other again. Every time I flew to Louisiana for a signing, my sister would leave town. Knowing she couldn't stand to be in the same parish with me stirred a mix of emotions. Hurt, yes, but also (I'm embarrassed to admit) satisfaction. My memoir had apparently shamed her for what I believed at the time was wrongful behavior. I'd told my side of the story, vented my anger, exposed the injustice. But this kind of self-righteous gloating only deepened the chasm between us. And it hurt me as well. All the healing writing my book had brought me was clouded by guilt.

• • •

ANOTHER SISTER, MY YOUNGER ONE, celebrated her 40th birthday in 2004. She invited her six sisters and their families to join her on a Caribbean cruise. When she told me my estranged sister was going, I bowed out. I didn't want to make the trip awkward for anyone. After a few calls back and forth on our behalf, we both agreed to attend and behave like civilized adults.

The day my sons and I boarded the ship, we rounded a bend and nearly collided with said sister. My heart did a triple somersault. I greeted her with a smile and a hello, but was too afraid to hug or touch her. Then I introduced my sons. At this moment, I feared she'd simply come on this trip to tell me in person how despicable I was. But this was not the case.

Before setting out on this venture, I remembered something one of the river rafting guides had told me: "These trips are a mixed bag, a gathering of total strangers with different views and backgrounds. You never know who will end up in your boat. The trick to getting along is to just accept your boat mates, suspend judgment, and know that this isn't forever. Don't try to control anyone."

I kept this in mind as we sat down to dinner each evening and small-talked by the swimming pool. We slowly got to know each other again, and I felt a door open I'd long feared forever locked. We took a risk, set aside our differences, and baby-stepped down the path from resentment to forgiveness.

My sister had her own milestone birthday last year, and I helped organize the surprise party. When she entered the private dining room and saw me standing among her friends and family, she shouted, "Ma-ree, what the fuck are you doing here?" I smiled as she made her way over then hugged me.

Her forgiveness still amazes me. After what I'd revealed in my book, it's incredible that she treats me like family again. After this trip, I realized I still had a lot more forgiving to do. I had to forgive myself.

BLACKIE & ME

YEARS AGO, MY NEIGHBOR Amber asked me to check on Blackie, her cat, while she was away for a week in July. She gave me a set of keys to her garage and the vet's number. I accepted the job with much hesitation. Up to this point, I'd never owned a cat, except for a stray I once adopted then returned to the pound days later.

"He's got plenty of food and water," she said. "Just stop by periodically to say hi. Make sure he's okay."

I pictured a mass of black fur dashing past me the instant I opened the garage door. "Will he try to escape?" I asked. The idea of trying to corral one cooped-up cat and my two small boys as they all darted from one scratchy juniper bush to the next didn't appeal to me. Life as a divorced mom and struggling writer was already hectic enough.

"No, no," she assured me. "He's a laid-back cat."

"Then don't worry about a thing," I said, trying to assure myself more than her.

I set the key and the emergency contact on the antique secretary in my entry way. The next morning, I passed these reminders of my responsibility on my way out the door to grab the newspaper. My boys were waiting for me in the den watching cartoons. The cat was waiting as well, all alone in the dark of Amber's garage. Right after lunch, I told myself as I sneaked past the key, I'll stop by and say hi.

Later, as my boys napped, the doorbell rang. Sitting on the front step was a UPS package, a book I'd ordered. Before I closed the door, I thought, You really should go over now. Instead, I sighed. I didn't want to bother with the cat during my one peaceful break in the day. I'd go later. Before dinner. Definitely. But later never arrived. Every time I'd glance at that key or at Amber's garage, I'd panic.

My anxiety over the cat grew. At least a couple of times a day I'd pack my boys into their car seats and drive past Amber's house, telling myself that at the very least I should make sure he's fine. Or call someone. Ask another neighbor to check on him. But how would I admit my freakishness to the pilot's wife or the home-schooling mom without feeling immense shame? I kept picturing the abandoned cat, sitting quietly on my friend's workout bench, all alone in the summer heat, dejected, frightened. What if he died under my watch? I was a terrible friend.

Soon my guilt transformed into anger. What kind of person leaves a pet locked up in a garage in the middle of a heat wave anyway? If Amber didn't care enough about her stupid cat, then why should I? I'm not even a cat person. If he were mine, I would have at least sprung for a cat motel, sent him a postcard.

The rage then turned on me. Am I really such a wuss? A heartless and pathetic human being?

When I couldn't take it anymore, I split from reality. This was a survival tactic I'd taught myself in childhood, and sometimes I still relied on it. Often when my parents fought, I'd go off on an adventure in my mind. No longer would I be in my bed listening to the name-calling. I'd be in a tree house eating coconuts like the Swiss Family Robinsons. Left alone for hours at a time as a kid, held hostage by a fractured leg in a heavy cast, I fantasized that everyone had vanished. Gone. Dead. All my siblings and parents. No more rejection. No more *I don't have time for you right now.* Just me and the maid. She could take care of me until I walked again. Plus, I was self-sufficient. I knew how to boil corn, make baloney sandwiches, scoop ice cream into enormous bowls. When I needed money, I'd just sell off the art, the piano, the cars, the antiques. I had it all figured out. I could survive alone.

Now I created a fantasy about the cat: Wasn't that Blackie I just saw hunting critters in Amber's yard? There, look, he's under the willow tree. Hurray! He found a way out. He's getting some fresh air. Now I don't have to worry about checking in on him.

On day four, I walked outside as usual to get the paper and once the guilt hit, I conjured Blackie chasing a squirrel up the neighbor's tree. Look, now he's wrestling with a white kitty, they've got each other in a head-lock. Isn't that Blackie munching on grass again?

On Sunday afternoon my doorbell rang. It was Amber with a plate full of freshly baked oatmeal cookies. I froze.

"Thank you so much for checking on Blackie."

"Oh, yes," I said. "Won't you come in?"

We sat at my kitchen table and I removed the plastic wrap from the still-warm cookies. "You really shouldn't have gone to the trouble," I said.

"I just wanted to express my appreciation."

"No, really. There was no need." She glanced over toward the den. "They're napping," I said, figuring she was looking for the boys. Her blue eyes then settled on me. I knew I had to fess up, even if it meant she might never speak to me again. "Thing is . . ." I gulped. "I didn't go over. Not even once."

Amber cocked her head and set down the cookie she had just cracked in two.

"I couldn't bring myself to do it. I'm a freak, I know. I'm so sorry. I hope he's okay."

"Makes sense now."

"What's that?" I was waiting for the name-calling.

"Blackie must have gotten pretty pissed off. He scratched up the legs of the foosball table and crapped all over our work-out rugs."

"Ew." I grimaced. "But otherwise, he's okay?" She gazed out the window as if she were too disgusted to look at me. "I understand if you hate me." Then I told her how I'd convinced myself that I'd seen Blackie on the lawn, chasing squirrels, and playing with his feline pals.

I couldn't explain my behavior until months afterward when it occurred to me that I had been identifying with Blackie. I'd waited hours and sometimes days, in both childhood and adulthood, for someone—parent, friend, lover—to remember that they were supposed to come for me. I'd felt this abandonment when a boyfriend would disappear for days or weeks without a word, leaving me in the dark wondering what I'd done wrong, just like Blackie.

"But the door was locked. That's why I gave you a key."

"I have an active imagination," I said.

In her amazing capacity to forgive, Amber told me not to

worry about it. What's done was done. The cat had survived. We'd all learned a lesson. We ate cookies while she told me about her trip. I asked if she had any other travel plans.

"I'm going to Paris with my some of my women friends," she said. "I've got to find someone to get my daughter to school and back while I'm gone."

"I'm much better with kids than cats," I said.

We both laughed.

"Think I'll find someone else."

"Yeah. I probably would too."

LETTING GO

L ETTING GO OF RELATIONSHIPS that have passed their prime, that no longer enrich my life, has always been one of my greatest challenges. But if a friendship carries a lot of history—say, we met in a new moms' group and our children have known each other since before they were weaned; or we finished graduate school together; or we took our first writing classes, edited each other's manuscripts, encouraged each other through all the rejections; or we spent one weekend each August, for three consecutive years, backpacking through Desolation Wilderness, lying in sleeping bags outside our tent to watch shooting stars and talk about first loves, worst times, and everything in between; or we volleyed the same crazy, ego-centric boyfriends back and forth, consoled each other through each failed romance, supported each other through the deaths of our parents, and were right there each time the other said, "I do"; or we grew up in the same unstable household, shared our friends as well as our toys and clothes, and when it seemed unsafe to turn elsewhere, we were always there for each other—these relationships are precious to me. I hold onto such connections like a child clings to her favorite blanket, no matter how threadbare, stinky, or gross it might become.

"Friendships, like most things," my therapist would say, "have their life cycles. There's a beginning, middle, and end. Sometimes, just when you think they're dead, they're rejuvenated. Or they're reincarnated in a different form. Sometimes they're just done."

I understood this intellectually, but I refused it emotionally. One thing was certain, however, the harder I tried to hold on to these dying friendships, the more frustrated, isolated, and hurt I became.

From a hotel in Tempe, Arizona, where I was staying for the 2007 A's Fantasy Baseball Camp, I phoned my friend Lisa who lived in Phoenix. For two weeks prior, I hadn't been able to pin her down for dinner plans, despite her assurances she definitely wanted to get together. Now she was whining about the traffic, said she'd already started fixing dinner, was frazzled.

"But you knew I was coming in today . . ." I whined back. "It feels as if I'm the only one here making an effort."

After accusations flew back and forth, and even tears on my part, Lisa finally said, "If I'm always hurting your feelings, why do you want to be my friend?"

The obvious answers were that I wanted to meet the little Russian girl Lisa and her husband had recently adopted. I wanted to celebrate with Lisa that she finally had the child she'd prayed for her entire adult life. But even more, I just wanted to see my old college pal. A friend who could always make me laugh. Someone who got me. And I her. We're both smart, creative, capable, yet we possessed ditzy blonde, Southern sides as well. We could be narcissistic as hell and as generous as the heavens. We knew each other's parents before they died. We understood the futile hope for unconditional paternal love. Besides, who but I could attest to her hole in one in Kauai? Who walked up and down the beach with me on my honeymoon when I confided I felt like I'd made a huge mistake? We had laughed until our bellies ached when Lisa accidentally burned her cousin's truck down to its metal skeleton. Or when she straddled the bathtub in a pair of tight jeans and checked her reflection in the mirror before a date to go horseback riding with some cute guy.

Some of my fondest memories include the times we spent together in New York, San Francisco, New Orleans, Kauai, Gulf Shores, Los Angeles, Phoenix. We'd told each other almost everything. Sure, we'd squabbled, a couple of time even argued over the same man, but we always made up. I loved her like a sister. And I didn't *need* another sister.

So why did I want her to be my friend? I could have said, "I'm scared to let go. I'm scared that if I walk away, you'll never seek me out again. The distance and silence will grow until we finally slip away from each other's lives permanently." Instead, I played the victim through my tears: "If you really wanted to get together, you would have set aside time for me. I would do the same for you if you came to Walnut Creek."

She reminded me that she was now a married woman. Her husband came first. As a single person, maybe I'd forgotten that marriage required compromise, it came with obligations, and that often meant she couldn't just drop everything to hang out with *me*.

"I was married for six years," I wanted to say. "I know what's involved. It's not as if my life isn't complicated, too. I'm a goddamn single mother."

Lisa and I didn't see each other that visit. I never met her daughter.

After she left a couple of harsh phone messages, I finally suggested that we wait for a better time. But I thought about her often during Fantasy Camp and considered her question: "Why do you want to be my friend?"

I thought about how similar making time for meaningful friendships is to making time for physical exercise. What motivates me to get my lazy ass off the couch may not move another. When I'm exhausted, depressed, or under a lot of stress, I'd rather stay home, take a nap, read a book, or go see a movie. But I tell myself: Once you move your body, you'll feel much better. I know realistically that one skipped dive lesson or afternoon of softball won't make a difference, but I also know the longer I stay away and let my muscles laze about, the more likely I'll never go back.

By the time I returned to Walnut Creek, my ill feelings had subsided. I accepted that my friendship with Lisa had hit a dormant period. Maybe it will thrive again, I told myself. Maybe not. But for now, it was clear we needed a break.

One of Lisa's comments stayed with me. She said I was always worried or angry my friends didn't have enough time for me, and in a way, this had become a self-fulfilling prophesy. She was right.

I now realize that I can't force myself on others. I can't make anyone love me. But I can love myself. In fact, I have to.

TO HELL WITH THE
NAYSAYERS

T HERE'S ALWAYS AT LEAST ONE naysayer in the crowd. For some reason, this cynic wants to drag everyone else down, too. It's as if his day isn't complete, or sufficiently miserable until he's leveled the playing field.

On New Year's Day 2006, I was at a potluck dinner party. The host, an internist, and I were talking. I told him I'd signed up for the A's Fantasy Camp held later that month in Phoenix.

"That's crazy," he said. "Do you have any idea how fast those guys throw the ball? Upwards to eighty miles an hour. And I'm sure a lot aren't accurate. You're going to get hurt. I really advise against it."

Not once did he say, "Wow, sounds like fun. Didn't realize you liked baseball that much. I'd love to do that. You'll have to tell me all about it."

I left the party that evening fearing I'd spent four thousand dollars on a vacation that might end up permanently maiming me. My biggest worries about the camp, up to this point, had been whether or not the white polyester uniform would make my ass look humongous and if I'd meet any cute men from the Bay Area. (I always tell guys, "If you want to meet girls, think ballet, cooking classes, cheerleading camp, springboard diving, yoga. Go where the odds work in your favor.")

I suppose getting pegged by a baseball had crossed my mind. But there were risks associated with every sport, both in playing and watching. Hell, I could be munching away on a hotdog at Pac Bell Park one minute and the next have the imprint of a foul ball tattooed on my temple. Living fully meant accepting certain risks.

For the next couple of days, I reconsidered the Fantasy Camp. Maybe he was right. Perhaps the risks were too great. I should go skiing in Whistler instead. But I'd been looking forward to playing ball under the sunny Arizona skies with sixty men! And practically speaking, the organizers wouldn't allow women to enroll if the risks were too great. The brochure had basically said, "Come one, come all." Many of the players, I figured, were Sunday softballers, like me. Besides, Dave Henderson and his cohorts would be out of business by now if every woman who attended camp was wheeled off the field on a stretcher. I'd take my chances.

At the opening reception, our host, Dave "Hendu" Henderson introduced the Camp's staff and coaches: "Blue Moon" Odom, Greg Cadaret, Bert "Campy" Campaneris, Michael Davis, Carney Lansford, Art Howe, Shooty Babitt, and Tony DeFrancesco. After the coaches received their applause from the campers, the players all introduced themselves. A camper seated beside me explained that he'd returned after Googling himself and finding his 2005 Fantasy

Camp stats. Nervous and eager to fit in (so many of the veteran campers already knew each other and had formed cliques), I figured sex would be a sure-fire ice breaker. So I said to this roomful of strangers, "I'm Marie Etienne from Walnut Creek, California. And like him . . . " I nodded to my right, "I've *Googled* myself." The playful lilt in my voice, I had hoped, would suggest more than an Internet search.

After the laughter subsided and the older men exchanged baffled looks (i.e., *Should she really be admitting that in mixed company?*), I added, "I'm here because I came home one Friday night and found an e-mail from the A's inviting me to their Fantasy Camp. I figured what the heck, sounds like fun." I stopped short of saying the deciding factor was knowing that most of the participants would be male. What better place for a 43-year-old divorced mother of two to chase sixty grown "boys" in tight white pants around the bases?

Before leaving for Arizona, if I'd heard the term "Kangaroo Court," I would have envisioned a bunch of furry marsupials thumping around with a basketball in the outback. Now these words carried a different meaning: team building, laughter, accountability. "Court's in session," Greg Cadaret said each morning in the A's training room. "Please stand for the Honorable Shooty Babitt."

"You got thin skin," Shooty warned at the outset, "might as well leave now." No one was above the law of our Chief Justice. Every morning we waited to see who the witty, irreverent Shooty would call up on charges. Token fines and credits were levied in fun and to keep us on our toes. Shooty ribbed and reprimanded the umps, coaches, equipment manager, and trainers as well. When an ump let Coach Mike Davis talk him out of a legitimate call, he was charged a buck. On day two, I was brought before the court for mistaking the men's locker room as a shortcut to the field. When Shooty asked if I'd *Googled* myself after seeing the guys in their jock straps, I blushed and said, "Unfortunately, the stench in there had the opposite effect on me." My comeback earned me a dollar credit with the understanding that I'd reciprocate to the guys by modeling my underwear in the training room. A quick flash at Shooty on the last day helped me avoid further fines.

Everyone was held accountable. If a batter tossed his bat after striking out, it cost him seven dollars. "One for each day you've forgotten to take your meds." If you missed a routine play at second, be ready to plead your case and accept the fine. Wear a shirt more garish than the previous day's and earn one credit. Your girlfriend shows up in a low-cut halter top . . . "Another buck for the man!" When the wife complains that the only thing hard in the hotel room was a frozen Snickers, get out your wallet.

Even if we hadn't played a single game the entire week, the laughter and camaraderie would have made the trip worthwhile. However, we did play usually two games a day. And in the finale, campers versus pros, I knocked a double into left field off former All-Star "Blue Moon" Odom. I drilled the first pitch over third baseman DeFrancesco and Blue Moon called "time" to give me a hug and the souvenir ball.

By the end of camp, many players were moaning in the hot tub, limping around the training room in ice-pack diapers, or slouching on the bench, massaging the aches in their buttocks and arms. A couple of men, as my internist friend had warned might happen, incurred injuries that required hospital visits. Although I deflected one wild pitch heading straight to my helmet by sticking out my elbow, my injuries merely consisted of a few bruises, a swollen hand, a jammed thumb, and acute humiliation.

Which brings me to "Bill." I didn't connect with my fantasy man as I'd secretly hoped. It seemed that most men who spend thousands of dollars to attend a weeklong sports camp don't do it with the goal of meeting women, but rather for that male bonding experience: to spit tobacco, adjust their cup, drink beer, and play ball from morning till midnight. However, all week long, this married guy Bill and I harmlessly flirted. Is there really such a thing as *harmless* flirting? Not really, but I assuaged my guilt by telling myself I didn't intend to take it beyond verbal foreplay.

It was clear that Bill saw a lot of leeway (I love the Oxford definition of leeway: "allowable scope of action") within his marriage vows. I stated several times that I wasn't interested in a fling. But we joked about how I kept giving him mixed messages, not the least of which was the note I left at his door on the last night: *So you're not going to tell me good-bye?* I didn't intend to do anything. Really.

At 2 a.m., my roommate and I were asleep when a tap on the door woke me. I knew it was Bill. I knew he was lit up after carousing the Scottsdale bars. And he was probably horny. Most men are when they come knocking on your door in the middle of the night. Figuring he'd go away if I didn't answer, I lay there and waited. He knocked again, then again, even louder. Finally, I slid out of bed, quietly closing the door separating the bedroom and the living room, and greeted him.

I could smell the scotch on his breath, but he wasn't falling down drunk. He had something black draped over his arm.

"I didn't get a good-bye hug," he said and stepped into the room. "I brought you a gift to remember me." He held up a monogrammed A's Fantasy Camp sweatshirt, which I knew cost a ridiculous amount of money.

Suspicious I hadn't really been the intended recipient of this gift, I said, "That wasn't necessary. And quiet. My roommate's sleeping. You shouldn't even be here."

"One kiss and I'll leave."

"Thought you came for a hug."

"I'll take that too."

I stood on my toes and gave him a quick peck on the lips. "There. Now go. I'll see you at breakfast."

"Don't you want to try on the sweatshirt?"

I held it up to my chest and said, "See . . . it fits. Now go."

"I like your pink PJs. They're kinda sexy."

"And you're kinda drunk. Out of here."

"One real kiss and I'll leave."

He bent down and when our lips touched, he instantly pulled me closer. The second his tongue slipped into my mouth, I knew we'd crossed the line between emotional infidelity and the real thing.

Feeling myself respond to him, I pulled away. "Thanks for stopping by but you've definitely got to go."

He took my hand and I assumed he'd kiss it, but he pressed it against his crotch. "Feel the hard-on you've given me." I thought, Is this love? "Can't we just kiss a little longer? I promise—"

"No. Shu."

"Can I just touch your breasts?"

I grabbed his hand and set it on my right boob for a heartbeat, like a middle-schooler. "There. Happy? Out of here."

He took a step back and knocked a coffee mug off a nearby table. I cringed at the noise. My roommate was a very conservative, religious woman who had told me she considered infidelity an unforgivable sin. I ushered Bill out the room then crept back to bed. An hour or so later I woke up and saw a light under the door leading to the living room. My roommate's bed was empty. Within minutes I was dreaming again.

When the alarm went off I looked around the room. Her bed was empty. Her bags were gone. She wasn't in the living room or taking a shower. I figured she must have been eager to get an early start.

When I saw her standing in the lobby with some of the other players I waved. She turned away as if she hadn't seen me. I walked over and said, "Good morning. I enjoyed rooming with you and hope to see you again at the reunion game."

She gave me a half-smile and turned to one of the other players. The guys looked everywhere but at me.

At the airport I searched for her and finally found her standing apart from the others players who were on our flight. I approached. "I'm sorry if we woke you last night. A player stopped by to give me something. I know it was late."

She didn't look at me. "I don't want to talk to you. Go away."

Shocked, I mumbled, "Wow."

"Wow is right. Now leave me alone."

She huddled with a group of the veteran campers who apparently weren't talking to me either. I returned to my seat, my heart pounding. I couldn't even walk the distance to the bathroom to decompress in private for fear I might cry. I sat in my chair staring out the window at the tarmac.

I couldn't stop the paranoia: Had she told everyone at breakfast? Would I be remembered as the team slut? I didn't want to be blackballed from ever attending the games again? Maybe I'd get a special plaque in the men's locker room.

As I processed what had happened, I admitted I'd used poor judgment. I had screwed up. But that didn't make me a dirty whore. Of course, I never heard from Bill again. It clearly wasn't love.

Months later, I attended the reunion game and barbecue in Oakland with much trepidation. I'd heard from a player that my former roommate had indeed spread the word of my indiscretion. I brought Austin and Zack along as a buffer. She'd see that my sons were well-adjusted boys, I wasn't a total loss of a mother, and I'd avoid a confrontation. But when I saw her talking to the organizers, I panicked. What if she came over and told Austin and Zack that their mother was a tramp? Or what if we're seated in the same row and they overhear her talking about me to another player? I steered the boys to the buffet and didn't complain when Zack filled his tray with two hamburger buns (no meat), chips, and a soda. Every time my former roommate got within ten feet, I'd usher the boys in a different direction to meet someone else. She did the good Christian thing anyway and just ignored me.

For months after this experience, every time I thought about how hurt and humiliated I felt at her rejection, anger and shame would rise up inside of me. I had once again allowed myself to be used by a man for momentary pleasure. And I used him. I didn't have enough self-respect to stop the flirtation early on or to wait for a more appropriate (i.e., single) guy. Once again, I'd shortchanged myself and chased the wrong tail in the pursuit of happiness.

When the enrollment forms arrived for the 2007 season, I initially thought there was no way I could face the coaches and players again. Little Miss Righteous was a repeat attendee and I had very little doubt she'd return. A close friend to whom I'd confided advised against my returning. She said I was crazy to even consider going back. Why not check out the Giant's camp and start fresh? She had a point. But then, screw Miss Righteous! Yes, I did the wrong thing. It couldn't be undone. But I'd apologized. And I wanted to play ball with Dave Henderson and his gang. I'd worked hard to improve my game this past year. I figured I'd let the bitch hang on to her resentment for all eternity if that made her feel superior, but I wouldn't let her win by scaring me off.

At the opening reception, instead of introducing myself with a sexual joke, I figured I'd poke fun at my parenting. "I'm thrilled to be here for my second camp," I said. "My sons think I've gone out for a quart of milk. I'm hoping they don't notice my absence till next Sunday." My joke got the laugh I wanted, and besides the constant worry of having actually left my sons with an inexperienced babysitter, the week was off to a good start.

Miss Righteous and I managed to avoid acknowledging each other, despite having adjacent lockers. She would gear up first, then right before morning court, I'd change into my uniform. When our opposing teams would meet on the field after a game to trade high-fives, she'd simply bypass me. The public rejection hurt, but I'd remind myself that only a childish hypocrite would be so unsportsmanlike.

Divine retribution came unintentionally. Throughout the week, the players and coaches kept mixing up our names. In Kangaroo Court and in the dugout, they'd often refer to her as Marie and vice versa, no matter how many times she corrected them. I'd laugh to myself, knowing how it must have pissed her off to be confused with the camp slut.

In preparation for 2007, I'd gone to the batting cages and improved my in-field play. But still I found that hesitant players, like myself, ones who sit by quietly without complaint, were the ones pulled off the field in a close game. Whenever I was benched, I'd fume. This is Fantasy Camp! While the brochures had promised a true-to-life pro ball experience, and sitting the bench was a part of baseball, I had paid four thousand dollars to get my uniform dirty.

As the week progressed, I noticed that I sat out an average of three innings per game. The other two players who shared the bench with me were less skilled than the men who rarely, and sometimes never, sat. Soon it became clear: you pay you play, unless you're a woman or a really shitty player. As my team's losses stacked up, my coaches devised a nice way of yanking me off the field: "Marie, hang here this inning. Keep us company."

So here's some advice: When you're finally put in the game, don't dilly-dally in the dugout between innings. Grab your glove and head out like your pants are on fire. You're less likely to be grabbed by the jersey if you're already on the field. And even if you take a ball to the face and your lips swell ten-fold, no crying or whining about throbbing teeth or bleeding gums.

What did eventually bring on tears and a fear that perhaps I wasn't cut out for the Fantasy major leagues? The final game, campers versus pros. If you're not really into baseball, and the rare experience of playing on a major league field against men whose million-dollar careers earned them World Series rings doesn't make you want to do cartwheels in the manicured grass, then you might not understand my frustration. But a team without a manager means a free-for-all: no batting order and a race for prime positions. I desperately wanted to play. Each team was given three innings against the pros and I didn't want to sit on the bench. Judging by the infrequent hits the other teams had managed to get off the pros, we seemed to have a remote change of batting through the lineup before making the ninth out. So if I was last in the order, I might not get a chance at the plate. Or so I feared.

Although we agreed to keep the same order as the last game, some men began cutting in line. One guy switched teams right before our game, then decided he'd switch back so he could play a second game. When I complained, the guys looked at me as if I was a selfish bitch. One said, "Give him a break. He's traveled all the way from Australia." I wanted to say, "I may not have flown halfway around the globe, but I had my own hoops to jump through to make this camp. I'm a single mom with two children in school that need to be looked after."

He took his place at the back of the queue and I batted. I managed to get a hit and with the next batter advanced to second. The one after him hit to left field and I ran to third. When I reached the bag, the ump called me out. But the third baseman didn't have possession of the ball. It wasn't a pop-up where I'd forgotten to tag up. I figured the ump was trying to trick me like last year when Shooty asked me to step off second for a minute so he could clean the bag then tagged me out. So I stayed put. But the pros were now waving me off the field, insisting I was out, and yet my teammates were telling me to stay on the bag. Flustered, I didn't know what to do. Had I missed an out? I finally left the bag when my teammates began fetching their mitts.

By the time we shook hands with the pros, I was choking on tears. I ran from the field, crying hysterically with my teammates calling after me, "Come back, Marie. Let's do that *cheer thing*." They'd teased me all week when I'd referred to a rally cry as a cheer thing. The aftermath of pros, players, and staff trying to calm me down and figure out why I was so upset was more embarrassing than being snubbed by my former roommate. I was a grown woman crying over *baseball*.

Weeks passed before I realized that most men (and many women) would do whatever it took to get more play time, more chances at bat, and unless, as a woman, I was willing to assert myself, I'd be frustrated, resentful, and warming the bench. Simply playing the victim or thinking that everyone's version of fair is the same doesn't cut it.

My friend to whom I'd confided about the first camp simply shook her head when I told her about my crying spectacle. "I think you're done there," she said. "Why put yourself through any more grief? Why embarrass yourself again?"

Stubbornly, I refused to accept this. A few months later, I received a registration package for Dave Henderson's Stockton Ports Camp. There would likely be many of the same players from the A's Camp and the same unresolved issues. I decided to contact the head organizer and explain why I'd been so upset and ask if it was reasonable to expect more equitable play time. In my email I said, "I realize now that I should have spoken up earlier in the week in Phoenix rather than let my frustration build."

The man wrote back a very apologetic letter, saying he wished I had said something at the onset. He gently added that it was difficult to rectify a situation unless it was brought to your attention and the main goal was to have fun while feeling as if you've gotten your money's worth. I agreed to assert myself in the future and signed up for the Ports Camp. I also promised myself that if it came down to it, I'd thump my coach on the noggin and say, "It's my turn. Put me in the game."

LETTING GO
II

SOMEONE ONCE TOLD ME THAT having faith is like believing in an ocean because you've seen the river. But I'm one who needs to see the sandy shore and white caps first.

Austin, Zack, and I were on a bike trail near our home in Walnut Creek. In response to his brother's taunts about being a baby, Zack insisted that I remove his training wheels even though I told him he didn't seem ready to go it alone. He couldn't maintain his balance. And each time he'd fall over and scrape another part of his body, I'd cringe and plead with him to let me put the wheels back on.

With Austin, I'd lucked out. He learned to ride a two-wheeler rather easily. A few instructions from my neighbor and some practice with his father was all it took. But Zack wasn't getting it and I couldn't figure out what to say or do to help him. When I'm scared or unsure about something, my first impulse is to try to rush through the experience as fast as possible while holding my breath. This strategy wasn't helping Zack. After a few more spills and more than a few tears, he abandoned his bike and looked at me as if blaming me for his failure. I stomped my feet and huffed, "It's not my fault. I'm trying to help you but you won't listen."

An elderly man approached. Apparently, he'd witnessed the last spill. Zack was crying and I was near tears myself. He'll never learn, I thought. He's going to fall and knock out his teeth. His father should be here instead of me. I looked at the man and sighed. "I just don't get it. What will it take to teach him to ride?"

The man smiled and said, "Patience." There was no condescension in his voice or on his face. He was simply a wise man who had seen both the river and the ocean.

Patience. I saw myself through this man's eyes. I was behaving like an angry bully, a fool. The entire adventure should have been fun, a confidence-building experience—for both my son and me—but instead it had become a chore and proof of our ineptitude: I was a bad parent and Zack was a baby.

"Thank you," I said as the man walked past us. "I'm sorry, Zack. I'm not making this very much fun, am I?" He shook his head and wiped his eyes.

"How about I try to teach him?" Austin said. He was only six or seven at the time, yet he sounded so sure of himself.

"That would be wonderful."

I stayed back with the bikes while Austin ran alongside Zack, holding onto his handle bars and seat until he finally said let go. Within a couple of days, Zack was riding like a big boy. My contribution to the process was simply letting go.

FLESH-EATING
BACTERIA

SITTING IN THE BACK SEAT of the car, Zack, now eleven, asked me, "Mom, when are you going to get another boyfriend?" We were on our way to pick up Austin from school. I turned off the radio and looked in the rear view mirror. His big blue eyes stared back at me.

"Don't know, sweetie. Dating is a lot of work and I'm so busy right now."

The truth was I didn't trust my judgment in men. I usually saw the red flags waving right in front of my face but, like a bull, I charged anyway. Knowing I was often the greatest saboteur of my own happiness, I figured I was better off alone. Happier, almost. And besides, the boys were entering their turbulent teens. They would need me now more than ever. There would be time for dating later when the boys went off to college.

"Why do you ask?" I said.

Zack, now biting his nails, mumbled, "I don't know."

"Yes you do. Tell me, please."

"Well . . . if you had a boyfriend then you'd have some-one else to hang around with. You wouldn't need to spend so much time with Austin and me."

I felt as if I'd swallowed a bee. My throat constricted with the sting. I knew Austin, now thirteen, had been trying to force more independence. But here was my youngest, my sweet little Zack telling Mom to basically get a life.

· · ·

INSANITY. DOING THE SAME THING over and over and expecting different results. Insanity. Dating the same men over and over. Expecting that *this* time I'd get the love I deserved.

When I started dating again after my divorce, I found mid-dle-aged men—my peers—were unlike the career-focused, tentative, twenty- and thirty-year-olds of my past. When older guys spotted a woman they wanted, or thought they wanted, they pounced with all five paws. But once satisfied, they'd lie around and fart all day till hunger, once more, prodded them to action. After a string of disappointing relationships with handsome, successful, gregarious, emotionally-immature old lions, I finally told myself I needed to find the proverbial "nice guy." Instead, in walked Troy.

My friend Lisa and I were dining in a popular bistro in Phoenix, laughing hysterically about a bizarre case of flesh-eating bacteria that had been linked to a well-known building in Louisiana. We heard a booming, James Earl Jones voice and looked over at a nearby table. An African-American man had just been seated and was talking with the hostess.

"I think he's my neighbor, Chili Davis," Lisa whispered.

"He played for the Giants. Should we go over and say hello? See if he remembers meeting me?"

"I'll think about it while I'm in the bathroom," I said and slid out of the booth. When I returned, I found Lisa sitting at the man's table. Her eyes moved in sync with her flying hands, a routine she employed after a couple of glasses of wine.

"Ma-ree," she said, copying Jimmy's and my father's pronunciation, "meet Troy. He played basketball with the . . ."

Troy stood up. His chest passed my nose and kept going another two feet. I looked up at his huge smile and shook his hand.

"Your friend Lisa here thought I was Chili Davis. I always thought I was better looking." A deep belly laugh rumbled forth.

"Please, join us," Troy said. "I was just about to order dessert."

I smiled. His voice was sexy. He was such a huge man, even his eyeballs looked as if they were twice the size of mine. While we waited for a slice of chocolate cake and three forks, he said he'd noticed us earlier, wanted to know what was so funny. We told him the flesh-eating story and again giggled at the absurdity of finding humor in such an unfortunate situation.

Troy pointed to the enormous diamond on Lisa's hand and asked if she was married. "Happily so," she said. "But Ma-ree's not. In fact . . ." Lisa invited Troy to her upcoming first annual fiftieth birthday party and suggested he be my date. And that was how it began.

Having grown up in South Louisiana, dating a black man was something I hadn't considered. Not that I wasn't attracted to African-Americans. But having done so many things in recent years that shocked or disturbed my family,

I figured I could now do pretty much whatever I pleased. Besides, my parents were dead so they wouldn't care.

Two weeks after Troy and I met, I flew to Arizona, as promised, for Lisa's birthday. On Saturday evening, while Lisa finished dressing for the party, Troy and I sat on her living room sofa and chatted. Her husband had gone ahead to the restaurant to greet the early arrivals. Troy mentioned how rude the security guard to Lisa's gated (and nearly all-white) community had been. "I should have given that motherfucking guard the truth," he said. "My dad was a heroin addict and my mom raised three children by herself."

I immediately thought, Oh shit, what have I gotten myself into? He said he'd done many risky, stupid things as a young adult, which had gotten him into a lot of trouble, but now, after nine years in the NBA, he'd gotten his masters in global knowledge management. He was a well-regarded, well-paid businessman who had traveled most of the world to teach Harvard-educated white men and women, heads of industry, how to gain competitive advantage. He knew this famous person and that. As I listened, I sensed that he was trying hard to sell himself. What wasn't clear was why. He was handsome and funny. Surely dating wasn't a problem for him.

"I don't want to coast on my fame," he said, fiddling with the hem of his slacks. "Some chicks just love that pro ball stuff. But I've done all that. I want to be known for my mind not my ball-playing years. That was another lifetime. I don't even tell people about my time with the . . ."

We were both adventure seekers, we determined. I told him about some of my favorite escapades and he told how he'd recently fulfilled a life-long dream: skydiving. "I pissed my pants," he admitted with a chuckle. "But I jumped."

When we arrived at the restaurant, I saw that Troy was the only person of color in the entire room filled with forty or so people, mostly local doctors, interior designers, and real estate professionals. Lisa took the 10 x 12 card I'd made for her—a collage of photos from the past two decades—to show her sister and nephew, who were standing near the gift table. Troy reached for my hand and brought it to his lips. Surprised by his kiss, I just smiled. I was certain that no matter how brave he was trying to act, he must have been uncomfortable.

"Let's do it," he said, in a slightly higher voice than usual.

As we headed to the bar, one of Lisa's stepdaughters came over to greet us. After I introduced Troy to this woman, he leaned over and whispered, "Should we tell her my secret?"

I looked at him, puzzled. "That you pissed your pants?"

"No, you knucklehead." He thumped me on my head. "You know. That I played pro ball."

"Oh. Yeah ..." I looked at Lisa's stepdaughter and said, "Troy played ball back in the nineties with the..." From then on, he found a way to fit his NBA career into every introduction.

After Lisa's party, Troy and I began trading calls and flirty e-mails. He'd phone two or three times a day to say he was thinking about me and to ask how my writing was going (he'd expressed great interest in my work, although in the four months we dated, he never did get around to reading more than the flap of my memoir). He claimed we shared many of the same aspirations: spending time with our children and a partner, traveling the world, pursuing our hobbies, growing intellectually and spiritually. He wanted to know everything about me, yet every time I started to tell him something, the subject fast-forwarded to sex. One second we'd be discussing my latest marketing plans for *Storkbites* and the next he'd be telling me how he wanted to lick my toes.

Though we hadn't yet slept together, Troy talked often about moving to the Bay Area. He claimed marriage was the next important step in his life. He'd never even lived with a woman, always putting his career first, but now he was ready to shift his focus. He asked often about my sons, joked about what Zack and Austin would say when they met this six-foot-seven giant of a black man. He claimed he could be a good father figure. "Tell them the basketball player says hi!" he'd say just before we hung up. His e-mails typically ended with something corny like, "I miss you and see you in my dreams . . . Love and kisses, Troy." Mine usually mentioned something about missing his pillow-soft lips, his full-belly laugh.

So here was another middle-aged man who couldn't go more than a few hours without talking to me. Here he was planning our future together. He also swore he hadn't had sex in a long time and sounded eager to do a little mattress dancing.

Still, Troy was different, I told myself. For one thing, he was black. Second, he was interested in anything psychological. He was willing to look at his past and current behavior and admit his mistakes and shortcomings.

Troy was intelligent yet not condescending, like some of the other successful men I'd dated. He'd talk at length about things like intermittent reinforcement schedules in the workplace and I'd say, "Yes, exactly." He was ambitious yet practical. He had a large, custom-built house in Paradise Valley, but gone were the sports cars. He was a Toyota man now. He said that all the money and fame in the world would mean nothing if he died alone. He'd achieved everything professionally he'd set out to do. Now he wanted to focus on finding a partner. We were in exactly the same place in our lives at the exact same time. And he "got me." I'd express some random thought that crossed my mind and he'd laugh and say, "You're not the usual deal. That's what I really like about you." When our conversations became tedious exchanges of who was going to do what to the other when we finally slept together, I'd suggest we move on to something more thought-provoking like current events, the Iraq war, and he'd oblige.

A few weeks after Lisa's party, Troy flew out to Walnut Creek. The first time we lay naked together in a hotel bed and I touched his penis, I said, "It's so black."

He laughed. "What did you expect?"

"Chocolate, I guess, like a Tootsie Roll."

"Darling . . ." he said in his best James Earl Jones voice. "This cock ain't no Tootsie Roll."

Every time Troy ended a corporate training, he'd call me from his hotel around midnight to tell me about the kudos *this black dude* got from all these successful white CEO's. And how even despite the pleasure he got from the standing ovations and requests for his autograph, he'd give it all up to be with me, to sleep next to me rather than alone in yet another rented room.

I hoped I had I finally met someone who wasn't scared of commitment, someone who'd treat me with love and respect. For four months, the relationship grew despite the geographical divide. But then after he'd promised to fly out for my birthday, a work emergency came up, and he was too wiped out to catch one more flight.

"To honor your birthday," he said, "I'm going to send you a really nice gift."

"I don't want a gift," I said. "There's nothing you can buy

me that I can't buy myself. I simply want to spend time with you, to feel connected again."

"Soon, baby. Soon. But in the meantime, be on the look-out for a special gift."

It had seemed suspicious from the beginning that at fifty Troy had never had a significant, long-term relationship. But he had his excuses. And I allowed myself to believe he simply hadn't met the right woman. Me. He often said how his priorities had shifted. He *wanted* to focus on building a relationship now.

What I got from Troy following my birthday was a week of silence. No gift, no card, not even a call. I mailed him a sarcastic thank you note for the special no-show birthday present. More excuses followed. More broken promises. Soon it was obvious the only difference between him and the other men I'd dated was his skin color, his pillow-soft lips, his size seventeen shoes, his black penis.

I eventually told him that it didn't appear he was ready for a relationship. Rather than continue to disappoint each other, why not simply call it a day? If he wanted to phone occasionally to chat, to share successes and failures, that was fine. He put me on the same mass e-mail list that included many of his clients (heads of big companies) and every few days he'd send out a cartoon or some inspirational quote he'd come across.

One Friday evening after midnight, he forwarded a penis joke that was both crude and derogatory towards women. I knew he'd probably gone out for dinner, had a few glasses of wine, "shot the shit" with one of his favorite bistro waiters, and had come back to his big house feeling lonely. He wanted to reach out to people but in a very safe, hands-off way. I hit reply and typed, "Funny joke. Do you think it might be a little inappropriate for your audience? Hope you're well. Love, Marie."

I didn't hear from him again until a year later. The subject line of the e-mail read: *Thinking Fondly of you~SURPRISE!*

Dearest Marie,

I've thought of you fondly and often recently. Please forgive me for being so out of touch. I've been traveling quite a bit here in the last several . . . they are paying me a hell of a lot of money, honey. Nice to know I'm in demand!

How is your writing going? What's up with your life, my dear? I think of you more than you might imagine and I just smile. I trust the boys are well and embellishing your life with unique experiences. I would cherish the idea of seeing you sometime soon to "chill" and catch up. Life is good but I've been a busy boy! Personal life has taken a "bath" and has been on "hold" for quite some time.

Need to get away here sometime soon for a well deserved respite. You are truly unforgettable honey! Miss ya . . . Love & Hugs, Troy

How does one explain such bizarre, delusional behavior? The strongest emotion I could conjure for this man was pity. And even sadder than his letter was that I responded with a lighthearted note, ending with: "Let me know if you're ever in the area."

• • •

ZACK'S SUGGESTION THAT I start dating again came months after this final correspondence. My son wasn't alone in wanting to see me with a boyfriend, a partner, someone to complement the life I'd created with my sons. But I seemed determined to resist my friends' and sisters' advice to find a *nice* guy.

Recently, I examined dating under a different light. It occurred to me that when I meet an intriguing woman and I want to add her to my list of close friends, I don't call every day, two or three times perhaps, saying things like, "Just wanted you to know I was thinking about you," and I don't project way into the future about all the fun and exciting things we'll do together. If I did, she'd no doubt ask herself, "What's this woman's problem? Didn't she have a life before me?" Then she'd run in the other direction unless her life was likewise empty.

Dating is obviously different from platonic friendships. With dating, all those thrilling hormones start churning and soon I'm obsessed with taking the relationship to the physical level. But this is wrong. Right?

NO MEANS
NO?

CREATIVE ARTS BOOK COMPANY in Berkeley, the original publisher of *Storkbites*, folded abruptly, and I felt I had no choice but to launch my own publishing company to keep my memoir in print. My friend Melissa, who retired as a corporate engineer to write full-time, e-mailed me during this stressful period.

"Some days (when I think I've lost my marbles for doing what I am) I read this. Thought it might speak to you, too.

"Alice Hoffman to Adelphi University's 106th commencement in 2002: 'You have to take a chance. What may appear to be the safe choice may be anything but. What appears to be the risk—the impractical decision—may be your destiny. If you are true to yourself, there's no way you can lose.' Love, Melissa."

My investment in *Storkbites* was huge, emotionally and financially. I'd spent four years writing and revising the book and tens of thousands of dollars to take classes and write full-time. I shopped my manuscript to agents and publishers for more than a year. Then I endured two years of dealing with a non-responsive co-publisher, Creative Arts. With numerous readings set up in both California and Louisiana, I found out from several stores that their ordered copies of my memoir hadn't been shipped. It had taken so much finagling to arrange these readings and now what was I to do?

On a dreary Friday afternoon, after dozens of unreturned phone calls and rescheduled meetings, I arrived at Creative Arts' office to see my publisher, Donald Ellis. His receptionist said he was at the DMV. We'd have to reschedule. I told her to call his cell and say I'd wait here all day if that's what it took. When he finally returned and invited me into his office, I sat down across from his cluttered desk and said in the most even voice I could produce, "I've got readings scheduled for the next few weeks and you're telling me you can't afford to print anymore books, books I've prepaid for in advance according to our contract. I've done everything I told you I would. I've gotten reviews, advertised in newspapers, mailed out thousands of postcards. All you had to do was print the goddamn books and ship them. But if you can't fulfill your end of the bargain, I will take my book back and publish it myself."

Ellis' office was packed with unframed paintings of nude women. Every one with legs wide open revealing a full beaver shot. Had they been halfway decent renderings, I wouldn't have wanted to slice his balls off. But he was a sorry painter and his models looked like a harem of dowdy retards.

Finally, he said, "That's probably a good idea. I think you should take over the publishing yourself. I'm done here. I'm closing up shop tomorrow."

I felt my heart sink as I sat there in his unkempt office in a crappy chair that went with the rest of his crappy, nicked-up furniture. I wanted to cry. I wanted to beg him to beg me not to take my book back. I wanted him to apologize for being such a prick of a publisher and swear to do better. Instead, he called his wife into the office and asked her to bring all the purchase order information from various book distributors so I could ship the books myself. What he didn't bother telling me was that purchase orders are not transferable. The orders were between Creative Arts and the other companies. If I filled the orders, Creative Arts would receive payment. Not me. Nor my new imprint, Alluvium Books.

The two decent things Ellis did were to sign over all the rights to *Storkbites* and give me the contact information for his printer in Berkeley. Two exhausting weeks followed. I created a logo for Alluvium and purchased a bar code, printed new books, researched distributors, completed applications, opened a bank account, and obtained a business license.

While I was busy setting up my independent press, word spread about the demise of Creative Arts. *The San Francisco Chronicle* began interviewing many of the orphaned authors, including me. Many had been scammed out of thousands of dollars. I'd been receiving a volley of e-mails from these other irate writers. They wanted everyone to pool their efforts and funds to pursue legal action against Ellis. Knowing that a class action suit could be lengthy, costly, and most likely futile, I decided to cut my losses and put my energy into dealing with my own book.

As soon as the *Chronicle* story hit, a large literary magazine publisher I knew phoned. "You're not seriously thinking about getting into this business?" Howard said. "That's a stupid idea."

I looked at Melissa's e-mail, which I had taped to my

computer and read every time doubts emerged. *"What appears to be the risk—the impractical decision—may be your destiny."*

"Yeah, what else am I supposed to do? Give up?"

"Well, you'll never sell any books."

"Actually, I just shipped two hundred copies to Barnes and Noble."

"You'll never get paid. It's a hand-to-mouth business. We're always the last one to get paid, if at all. You're wasting your time."

After I hung up, I imagined him sitting at his desk shaking his head. Idiot, he was probably saying to himself. Of course, he didn't know I'd worked in accounts receivable for years in another life. If it came down to it, I knew how to pry a payment out of a tight fist.

Less than two months later, on December 15, 2003, I received a check from Barnes and Noble. It was printed on their standard glorious green and white stock and made out to Alluvium Books. My company. They had even assigned me a B & N Vendor ID number. Immediately, I phoned Howard.

"Guess what I'm holding . . . a check from Barnes and Noble for $2,100.00. Isn't that cool!"

"Why don't you make a donation to my magazine? We're always in need of funds."

I chuckled because surely he was joking. But he wasn't. That was all he had to say. Despite his lack of enthusiasm, I knew I was a success. Perhaps that explains my response. "I'll write you a check," I said. "Will three hundred help?"

• • •

TWO WEEKS AFTER I TOOK on the task of mailing galleys to bookstores, I received two calls asking me to do signings in a couple of local shops. After a few more weeks, when I hadn't heard from other key independent bookstore owners, I phoned them. One man who held weekly author signings I'd attended over the years seemed annoyed I was even telephoning.

"I'm calling to see if you received the galleys for *Storkbites*?" I said. "And if you'd like to have me do an author event in your store?"

"No," he said.

"Uh, no you haven't received the galley or no you don't wish to have me read in your store?"

"Both. I won't be extending an invitation to you—now or ever. Thank you."

He hung up, and I sat in my chair staring at Melissa's quote. I wanted to rip it into a million shreds. Why was I humiliating myself like this? Why didn't I just move on?

Instead, I forced myself to follow up with other bookshop owners and event managers. I scheduled a half dozen more readings. Then, a few more. I put the one surly bookseller out of my mind. Until he telephoned. "I just finished reading the galleys to *Storkbites*," he said. "I loved it and want to invite you into the store to do a reading and signing."

If I hadn't recognized his voice from having heard him introduce numerous authors, I might have thought it was a prank call. But it wasn't.

I learned something valuable from this experience, which I keep telling myself whenever life beams me with a knuckle ball: No doesn't always mean no.

ICING

MY YOUNGER SON ZACK decided he hated middle school. C's, D's, and F's were making regular appearances on his class progress reports. His pediatrician and I suspected he was having difficulty dealing with the stress of two vastly different households. I knew from my own pre-teen years how hard it was to catch up when I'd fallen behind on my schoolwork, and I didn't want Zack to face the same struggles. To motivate him, I'd tried the reward tactic, the loss-of-privileges tactic, and the lecturing-till-his-blue-eyes-glazed-over tactic. My walking buddy, Lynne, suggested on one of our Thursday morning laps around the reservoir that I try getting up earlier on school days to spend extra time with Zack.

Though I'm not an early riser, I managed for a week to get out of bed at six and hang out with Zack after his shower. Together, we'd pack his lunch. He'd ask about my dreams and shake his head when I asked if he remembered his. We'd flip through his skateboard magazines and admire the young kids and their amazing aerial stunts.

One morning, I popped his favorite Pillsbury Orange Rolls into the oven and said, "I'm going take a quick bath. Frost the rolls when the timer goes off and remind your brother to take his vitamin."

About the time I'd lathered my hair, Zack cried out. My heart clinched into a knot when he said, "Stop. Let go. Ow!" Even from my side of the house, I could hear him wailing. There was a scuffle going on. I heard one of my sons being shoved against the utensil drawer by the other. Immediately I pictured all the sharp edges in the kitchen. The knives. The glass. I jumped out of the tub, wrapped a towel around myself, and nearly slipped on the tile floor in my race to the door. With my hair full of suds, I ran down the hallway screaming, "Stop . . . stop . . . God damn it stop hurting your brother."

I rounded the corner just as Austin slammed Zack against the edge of the sink.

"What in the fuck are you doing? Get away from him."

Austin stepped back. Zack's shoulders heaved as he sobbed. He wasn't the kind of child who turned on the tears to get attention. Rather, he'd do anything not to look weak.

I turned to Austin, and said, "What did you do?"

His arms fell to his side. The wounded look on his face said, Why's it always my fault? "He ate all the icing." He pointed at the pan of rolls, and to be honest, they were only minimally frosted, and the frosting was the best part. Zack's chin quivered as he blinked away tears. In his hands were a knife licked clean and the small plastic cup with only a smear of orange. "You're fighting over frosting. Holy shit . . . you're going to risk hurting your brother because he ate more than his fair share of some stupid icing."

I tried not to cuss in front of my children and was usually successful. But right now I wanted Austin to know how angry and scared I was. The next words out of my mouth were cut short by a coughing fit. Anytime I screamed, it irritated my throat. I managed to croak, "I'm going to finish my bath but there'd better be no more fighting."

All day while they were at school I thought about my behavior. How I'd screamed and cussed like a crazy woman. Like my mother. Then it hit me.

Before the boys began their homework that afternoon, I called a family meeting. We sat in the living room and I held a copy of *Storkbites*. I read them a scene from my childhood. I was eight. It was the year before my brother Chess was murdered. My mother and older sister were in the bedroom two doors down from mine. They were fighting. Or rather, my mother was beating up my sister and my sister was crying for someone to help her, to get Momma off of her. But not one door opened. Not one footstep rushed up the stairs, not even from my father's study. Everyone was too afraid to come to her rescue. Instead, we shivered in our beds and listened to Momma's fists hitting my sister and my sister's body hitting the wall.

When I'd finished reading the passage, I was trembling. The terror I'd felt in not knowing if and when my mother would let up was as real now as it had been back then.

Zack immediately said, "Why didn't you beat your mom up? I would have taken a bat—"

"Yeah," Austin interrupted, "I would've whacked her in the head."

They went on for a couple of minutes describing how

they would have incapacitated my mother. I laughed at their enthusiasm.

"I was scared shitless. Even as an adult, I didn't have the guts to confront her."

"But she was old. You could have taken her down," Austin said.

"Perhaps," I said. "I think from an early age she taught me I was better off to keep my mouth shut and take the beating. But my point is . . . when I hear you guys fighting, when I hear one of you crying for help, I'm eight years old again and I'm scared, I'm angry, but I'm not helpless anymore. I love you so much that I don't want to see either of you get hurt."

"I still think you should have taken her down," Zack said. "Gotten a gun and shot her." Austin nodded.

"Perhaps you're right. In the future, however, no more hoarding the icing."

LONDON-WALLS
FALLING DOWN

ACCORDING TO NEWTON, CHANGE of motion needs an external force. To get something going requires a kick in the ass. To stop what never should have started requires hitting a wall. In other words, no amount of simply wanting an object to move will set it in motion. There needs to be some force.

In my early forties, I dated a man I'll call Larry. When our thirteen-month relationship ended, I found myself crying to all my friends and family. It seemed there was no sane way to push past my depression. One friend recommended that I check out a personal growth weekend she'd once attended. The company's website indicated dates and locations worldwide. I chose Thanksgiving week since the boys would be with their dad, and London because I'd always wanted to visit. Larry always said we'd go there together.

A sign in the hotel lobby welcomed attendees. The woman at the registration table was doling out name tags. She had such an unnatural sweetness in her voice I wanted to tell her cut the crap, no one was that nice. She gave me a questionnaire to complete. It asked: Do you have the support of your family and friends and medical practitioner for attending this seminar? Do you have any medical conditions that intensive emotional work might aggravate? Immediately I thought, What in the hell am I doing here? The last question calmed me: What do you hope to get out of this week? Sanity, I scribbled. Help getting over a difficult breakup.

I returned the clipboard and located the restrooms. Once inside the bathroom, the odor of urine almost caused me to dodge back into the hallway. Walking past a row of urinals, I entered the third stall and locked the door. While peeing, I heard someone else enter, someone with heavy footsteps. Urinals? Oh fuck. I was in the men's room. I cut off the stream of pee then zipped up. "Pretend you don't see me," I said as I dashed past a man who had, thankfully, already taken aim.

As soon as I exited, I saw the universal female sign on the door across the hall. For weeks, I had been operating on a faulty auto pilot. Now, intruding on the men's room, what a lovely way to introduce myself.

In the waiting area, conversation hummed as people gathered. I love British accents. They remind me of my favorite entertainers: Hugh Grant, Rod Stewart, Emily Watson, Keira Knightley. Some attendees had formed groups while others, like me, stood off to the side. Repeatedly, I overheard, "Any idea what to expect?"

At 8:50 a.m., the doors to the ballroom opened and I followed a crowd of forty or so men and women into the meeting room. Three long tables stood in the back with sound equipment. Some of the staff members fiddled with the equipment while others organized papers or arranged pitchers of ice water and cups around the room.Chairs were stacked along the walls but the center of the room was empty. On the stage stood two tall director chairs and a podium. To the left a huge tablet hung from an easel.

A dark-haired woman wearing a business suit strode into the ballroom. The staff halted their tasks, faced forward, and applauded. It was as if the Pope had just emerged from her Pope Mobile.

The woman took the stage, stood poised like a principal ballerina, and waited for the applause to stop. She didn't fidget with the hem of her black jacket or shift from heel to toe in her pumps as I might if faced with a roomful of strangers. She had obviously done this dog and pony show before.

"Thank you. Welcome. My name is Kerri." A microphone was clipped to the collar of her blouse so that her voice was as clear and polished as her nails. She made deliberate, brief eye contact with one person then the next, her eyes moving around the room like the second hand of a clock. "I'd like to honor each and every one of you for deciding to change your life by being here today." She clapped her hands like a seal at Marine World.

"To get started, I'm going to ask Matt to put on some music while you walk around and say hello to your fellow participants. *Not* with words but with a smile or eye contact. No talking, please."

Bob Marley's "Lively Up Yourself" filled the room. I looked at the strangers I was to spend the next three days with and located the exit sign above the door we'd entered. Some of the people looked like a normal Jane you'd see at Macy's, and others, well, let's just say someone had cast a wide net over Great

Britain. I smiled at a multi-pierced, multi-tattooed biker then started moving in a clockwise circle with the others. Soon, the staff filled in among us, some of the nerd-looking ones swaying offbeat with the drums. It was easy to tell the staff from the participants: We mostly kept to the perimeter; they weaved freely among us. I returned a nod if someone came my way, but mostly I just fixed a smile on my face.

"Breathe," Kerri said. "Some of you look like zombies." Finally, she signaled for the music to stop. She again clapped her hands like a seal. "Well done. Grab a chair and make five rows." Once we were all seated, she asked each of us to introduce ourselves and say what had brought us there.

The sound guy and another man now stood on either aisle holding cordless microphones. The mikes traveled from person to person. Some, like me, were here to get over breakups. Others wanted to be more present in their lives. Others were caring for loved ones with terminal diseases, everything from AIDS to Parkinson's. One actor was drowning in debt, too afraid to tell his family. There were the recently divorced, recently widowed, recently fired, and recently empty-nested. Some said something was missing from their lives.

When I held the mike, I said, "I recently broke up with a man and I can't quit obsessing about him. I'm depressed. I figured rather than jump off the Golden Gate Bridge, I'd give this a shot."

I sat back down and quickly passed the mike as if it were a stick of dynamite. Kerri shook her head and her brown bangs shifted across her forehead.

"Please remain standing, Marie. Are you ready to transform your life? Are you willing to let go of the blaming, the anger, the should be's . . ."

I nodded like a first-day cadet at a swearing-in ceremony.

"Let's hear you say: 'I'm ready to transform my life. What I've done up to this point hasn't worked. I'm ready to try something new.'"

She repeated the prompt, then I said it with her.

"Now everyone stand. Say it with us . . . "

The hypnotic sound of our voices bounced off the white walls. I wanted to believe three days in this hotel conference room had more than one in a million odds of transforming my life. But I was skeptical.

"Are you as excited as me?" Kerri asked. Her eyes were wide open and the smile on her face now seemed genuine as people nodded and answered yes.

"Before we move on, let's give Marie a hand."

When the applause ended, she asked Matt to pass out the rules. We were asked to sign a contract promising that for the duration of the course we would refrain from using profanity (*fuck, asshole, God damn*, and *shit* were given as examples) and ingesting consciousness-altering agents or chemicals (alcohol, caffeine, tobacco, chocolate, or drugs of any kind unless prescribed by a physician). We also had to leave our cell phones, watches, candy, mints, gum, and beverages at the door. We were to speak only when acknowledged by a facilitator during the designated sharing periods and we had to remain in the training room unless granted permission to leave by a team captain. We weren't allowed to engage in sexual relationships with anyone in the seminar, and lastly, we needed to be seated in our chairs, and silent, by the time the leader entered the room.

There was grumbling among the participants. "You're treating us like children."

"Well, I'll sign," a man behind me said, loudly, "but that's no guarantee I won't go out and have a beer tonight." He crossed arms. It was going to be a standoff.

"Why would you give your word . . . which is what you'd be doing by signing the contract," Kerri said, "and then fail to keep it?"

"I don't see how one beer is going to make a difference?"

"Perhaps you don't." She stepped off the stage and approached the man. He sat back in his chair, uncrossed his arms. "Do you make a commitment knowing, even then, you won't keep it?"

He shrugged and scratched his curly brown hair. Kerri motioned for the staff person to bring over a microphone. "Stand up, please." He stood. His tenacity reminded me of Larry, whom I could imagine refusing to sign this document solely on the grounds that he didn't want to be told what he should and shouldn't do. "One of the purposes of this weekend is to notice the patterns of our behavior that get in the way of a richer life. Why do you think I'm asking you to sign this letter of commitment?"

"To control us. Exert your power over us."

There were a couple of snickers around the room. Kerri showed no sign she'd heard them. "Perhaps. Perhaps I'm a power hungry bitch and I get off on keeping you under my thumb." His face was still as stone. "And maybe you're thinking, 'Shut the fuck up, you cunt.'" The woman next to me gasped and then pressed on her temples. "Or maybe, I'm asking you to do something that, at times, might be difficult, might go against your normal routine, but might also help you stay focused on what it is you really want. All I'm asking is for you to commit that you will abide by these rules, no matter how ridiculous they might seem, and to keep that commitment until Sunday evening at nine p.m. After Sunday, you're free to go back to your old life. Can you do that?"

He smiled and signed the paper.

After this there was a bathroom break. I hid in one of the stalls for eight of our allotted ten minutes, applying lipstick, reading the graffiti in the stall. Upon re-entering the conference room we had to deposit cell phones and watches in a shallow wicker basket in accordance with our contract. Then Matt stepped onto the stage and applauded as Kerri entered the room. We were cued to follow suit with a welcoming gesture. We followed this protocol every time we reconvened.

"Before we get started," Kerri said, "stand up if you violated a commitment during the break?"

We were gone ten minutes for Christ's sake, yet a third of the attendees stood. On my row there were three people, including me, who remained seated. The door to the ballroom opened and a young, redheaded woman rushed to her seat. All eyes turned to her and she smiled.

"What commitment did you break?" Kerri asked, addressing this woman.

Red blushed. She mumbled, "I said fuck and I ate a chocolate bar. Also, I brought my cell phone into the room."

Kerri squinted. "Is that it? What about the fact you're late? Isn't being in your seat, ready to begin, one of the commitments you made?"

"Oh, yeah. Forgot."

Kerri placed her hands on her narrow hips and walked toward Red. *"Oh, I forgot.* Does that make it all right then? You're smiling. Do you think this is funny?"

Red's face turned white. I squirmed in my chair, thinking, What a bitch, what am I doing here?

After she'd finished with Red, Kerri went around the room asking people what rules they broke. The man who'd accused her of trying to control us with her rules was the last person standing.

"What rule did you break?"

He held the mike up to his mouth and said, "I went to the bar and had a beer?"

I laughed and soon realized that I was the only one who did.

"A beer. You had time to drink a beer in ten minutes?"

"I had time for two but figured one would take the edge off."

Kerri offered no rebuttal. She simply asked if he wanted to recommit and he did so.

"The purpose of asking for your commitments is to make you aware of how you interact in the world. I want you to stop and notice each action," Kerri said. "Ask yourself, Am I working toward a richer, fuller life?"

We were told to take out our notebooks and make a list of resentments. Everyone, everything, every situation that caused us ill will, we were to write on the left side of a page. She sat down on the director's chair and looked at her watch. "Twenty minutes. Start." Quiet piano music played in the background as I scribbled away in my book. When the timer beeped, Kerri asked who wanted to share a few items from their list. Immediately, the woman next to me raised her hand.

"I resent my parents and all their disappointments in me. 'Why didn't you finish university? Why did we go without for so long just to watch you drop out of school?'"

Kerri walked over, placed a hand on the woman's heaving chest. "Breathe. Let it out." When the woman finally composed herself, we clapped.

When it was my turn, I stood and said, "I dated this divorced man who claimed all he wanted was a woman to love him. And I loved him as hard as I could. Then he bought a Ferrari and decided he just needed to be alone. He loved me, he still claimed, but he didn't have the time or interest to date anyone. Two weeks later, he was sporting around town in his dumb Ferrari with some other woman. I resent the fact that he lied and didn't think my love was enough." Everyone clapped.

The next assignment was to pick one resentment either toward a person, persons, or issue in your life. "Don't hold back," Kerri said. "Confess the full magnitude of your resentment, and don't forget that you may have contributed to the situation as well, so add your thoughts and actions. You're free to spread out."

I scooted my chair apart from my neighbors. There was no mystery as to who I'd be writing to. For a half hour I scribbled away at an angry Dear Larry letter. When the timer buzzed, my hand ached and it felt as if the room had dropped twenty degrees.

"Now make two columns. Label the first column: Payoff. The second: Costs."

In red marker, Kerri wrote two sentences on the white board: *We get to feel superior. We get to play the victim.*

"Marie, you said a man promised to love you and then it turned out that he didn't. Or couldn't. And now you're hurt. In holding onto your resentment, what is the payoff? What do you get out of holding onto the anger?"

I looked at the white board. Matt handed me the mike.

"I get to play the victim. Look at poor me and how I've been hurt."

"Yep. There might be some feelings of superiority mixed

in as well. So what I want each of you to do is list the payoff next to each of your resentments."

I grabbed my pen and notebook. Starting at the top of the page was "Larry jerking me around." I marked V, S. As Kerri had said, I felt both victimized and superior, as in "I would *never* treat another human being this way!" Of course, this was bullshit.

Momma for abusing us. V

Daddy for ignoring her "visits" to our rooms. S, V

Managers for sticking me in right field or last in the lineup. V

My sons for always telling me that I should get a real job and quit wasting my time writing. V

When I came to the end of my long list, I looked up. Kerri was writing on the white board. *Resentment keeps us tied to the past.*

Scanning my list of resentments, it occurred to me how pointless these grievances actually were. How much time and energy had I invested in resenting these things, these people? What in the hell can I do about most of them now anyway?

"All right. Return to your chairs. Who'd like to share first?"

The man whose wife died of cancer raised his hand for the mike and stood.

"Feeling like a victim because the doctor said my wife had two years and it turned out to be only six months." He shifted his weight. "But I don't understand how identifying the pay-off here will actually help me to forgive."

Kerri applauded him and said, "All I ask, right now, is that you trust me."

The mike moved around the room and eventually came to me.

"Marie, what do you do when you're feeling resentful?" Kerri said. "Give me an example of a situation where you acted out your anger or hurt."

I stood up and took the mike.

"Recently, I sent *the* ex-boyfriend's key back and asked that he return mine." I paused and looked around at my fellow participants. "Sorry," I apologized, "another jilted-by-my-boyfriend story. After two weeks and no key, no response, I called him. He acted hurt. He couldn't understand why we had to give back each other's keys. I wanted to say, 'Because you're boinking someone else, you prick.' Instead, I told him I didn't trust myself with his key, that sometimes I wanted to let myself into his house and wait for him in his bedroom, and other times I wanted to sneak in and snoop through his drawers. Then when I was feeling really angry, I wanted to pour a bucket of red paint on his pristine beige carpet. Well, you can imagine, he didn't have much to say after that other than, 'I'll put it in the mail right away.'" The woman next to me snickered.

Kerri frowned. "So the payoff to resenting his holding onto your key is . . ."

"I get to strike back. Say, 'See how much you've hurt me. I'm so wounded and desperate that I want to destroy your carpet to get your attention.'"

"The payoff is that you get to be the victim. But what's the cost?"

"I'm not sure I follow you."

"In exchange for harboring this ill will and even acting out on it, what did you get? What was the pay off?"

"He'd know how much he hurt me. He'd feel guilty. Maybe he'd see how much I love him and want me back." I laughed at myself. "God, am I really that pathetic?"

"Yes. But you don't have to be." Fuck you, lady. "Go with

me here . . . I'd say the payoff was zilch. Nada. Only a huge cost. And do you know what that cost was?" I froze. "How did you feel after making the call?"

"Pleased for about a millisecond that I'd finally stood up to the jerk, then like a total idiot. I figured that whoever he was having lunch with when I called got an earful, a big laugh at my expense. So I guess, the cost was that I humiliated myself."

"Yep." She mimed an old-fashioned scale with her hands, moved them up and down. "Cost. Payoff. Cost. Payoff. Was there really any payoff?"

I lowered the mike and shook my head.

"I want everyone to look at their lists." She walked over to the white board and circled her earlier writing: *Resentment keeps us tied to the past.* "Ask yourself: Am I carrying an enormous backpack filled with resentments? Think about how light and free you'd feel if you just emptied your pack, took all the dead weight off your shoulders."

"But wait," I said, "If we let people crap all over us and we say, 'Oh, well . . . it doesn't matter,' aren't they just getting away with hurting us and everyone else who crosses their path? They'll never learn." My hands were trembling as I held the mike and waited for a response.

"And by God, we're here to teach them," she said. "We're here to save them from themselves. Hallelujah. Maybe they do come away unscathed. And maybe they don't. You don't know. You'll never really know so why worry about it. You can only change you." She pointed around the room. "You. You. You." Kerri printed in large capital letters the word PAYOFFS. I turned to a clean sheet of paper and wrote PAYOFFS at the top. The mike went around the room and Kerri wrote their responses. "You get to blame . . . Mask the hurt . . . Feel powerful . . . Revenge . . . Pity the other person . . . Form resentment-based friendships . . . Justification for acting inappropriate . . . Disengage . . . Act the martyr . . . Approval . . . Self-righteous." I copied down the list and saw they really weren't payoffs. A payoff was more like studying hard and getting an A, or forcing yourself to approach a bookstore owner and leaving with an order.

By Sunday morning, I was an emotional dishrag: limp, crusty, threadbare. I was ready for the shopping and dining portion of my London trip to begin. I slouched in the back row copying notes from the white board. Kerri had titled the column: Costs of Resentment. The mike had already made it down the first two rows. In my notebook, I'd written: "COSTS: Self-esteem, health, sexuality, self-expression, intimacy, creativity, spirituality, integrity, pain, shame, pressure, loneliness, hard-heartedness." As people ran out of labels, they simply offered anecdotal evidence of costs. Kerri, always the final word, would decide under which category these costs would fall.

When I took the mike, I said, "I still don't buy into this notion of resentment being entirely bad. If we harbor resentment, then yes, we have to face the associated costs. But if we're constantly forgiving or turning the other cheek, then there's the cost of getting trampled on over and over. Where does that leave our self-esteem?"

"Same place it was before the resentment-inducing event. You either have self-esteem or you don't. You either work to build it or you don't. Healthy self-esteem isn't dependent on another's actions. Right? Think of yourself as the CEO of Marie Incorporated. What one very important tool do you need to bring to work every day?"

"Self-esteem."

"Yep. Healthy self-esteem." Kerri hopped off her chair and walked over to the left side of the room. She moved the easel and faced the wall. Fists on her hips, she pulled her shoulders back. "Wall," she said, apparently addressing the wall, "I want there to be a door here." She walked straight into the wall and bounced back, pretending surprise. "But there's got to be a door here somewhere." Her hands moved up and down and in circles for an opening. "There should be a door!" She pouted and glanced at the audience. "What should I do?"

"Use a different door," someone shouted. Someone else suggested a jackhammer. Another hand shot up, and the lady said, "Accept the fact that it's not a door. It's an immovable wall."

Kerri shook her head defiantly. Once again, she approached the wall. But this time she sneaked up on it like one might a feral kitten. "Here, door. Please open up. Just for me. You said you'd be a door. Won't you please . . ." She stroked the wall as if it had feelings and was capable of responding.

She smiled, backed up a few steps, and tried again. But, of course, it refused to give. Tromping back to the middle of the stage, Kerri addressed the audience. "It's not fair. Why is the wall doing this to me? Don't I deserve a door?" There were chuckles around the room. Kerri folded her arms, studied the wall. Suddenly she screamed so piercingly loud I nearly jumped out of my chair. The sound of notebooks and pens slipping to the floor commingled with her shriek, "God damn it! Why won't you be a door!"

She ran toward the wall and slammed into it with her shoulder then bounced off, stumbling backwards and falling limply to the floor. That had to hurt. I imagined the look of horror on the hotel guests' faces as they headed to the nearby restroom and heard the commotion coming from our room. She pulled herself off the ground and stormed over. "Open now. Do you hear me? I want a door right here, right this instance. Don't make me angrier."

She waited as if by some magic a door knob would appear. When nothing happened, she began pounding her fists, screaming accusations and threats.

Okay, okay, I got it. I was Kerri. No amount of pleading, cajoling, yelling, threatening, or other inappropriate behaviors would change a situation. Sometimes you simply had to look elsewhere for what you needed.

• • •

THERE WERE DEFINITELY HOKEY moments throughout the weekend. Like walking around the room on Sunday evening at the close of the training, locking eyes and saying "I love you" to each and every person. Like sitting in our chairs with our eyelids closed, pounding on our thighs, repeating the words "I am enough." I left the conference feeling hopeful, but in the end, the hope was fleeting. It'd take more than a three-day seminar to knock down all the walls I'd built up over a lifetime.

IF

If you can keep your head when all about you
Are losing theirs and blaming it on you;

. . . .

If you can meet with Triumph and Disaster
And treat those two impostors just the same;

. . . .

Yours is the Earth and everything that's in it,
And—which is more—you'll be a Man, my son!

R UDYARD KIPLING'S "IF" was my father's favorite poem and yet I always hated its cautionary, tough-love advice. Buck up. Act like a man. No tears. No vulnerability. Kipling's maxims for life felt as biting cold as our backyard pool in January.

At age forty-three, I faced a series of blows: love lost, health threatened, friendships dissolved, and a shoulder injured. Rage and disappointment at how things *ought* to be turned inward until I found myself deeply depressed. I reached a point in my hopelessness where I'd kiss my boys good-night after story time, then lie awake wondering which would be the least painful, most successful means of killing myself: a graceful dive off the Golden Gate bridge? a sharp right turn off Highway 80? a razor blade? a fifth of vodka? that half-filled bottle of Tylenol with codeine from my last surgery?

One Sunday, my ex-husband dropped off our sons and mentioned they'd come home from school again on Friday broken down in tears, telling him how worried they were about me. They were scared to leave Mom alone on the week-ends. Mom was always crying and angry. Hearing how I was hurting my sons only added to my despair.

There came a point when I shut down. I quit sharing my suicidal fantasies with my friends and sisters and plotted in secret, rationalizing my plans by telling myself my boys would forgive me when they were older. It was in everyone's best interest. I made to-do lists of the things I needed to take care of before I died: discard embarrassing journals, update my will, create a trust for the boys, invite my closest friends over for a farewell dinner, visit my sisters one last time. It was such a relief to have something other than my own fears and misery to focus on. I could now put myself into the details of my death. It was like preparing for a big going-away party where I would be the guest of honor. *Good-bye, I'll have two slices of cake! See you all later . . .*

Around this time, Austin and Zack's relationships with their father and, in particular, their new step-mother began a rapid decline. They complained about not feeling welcome anymore at their father's house. It broke my heart to hear recaps of their horrible weekends. As things worsened for them, I realized that if I killed myself, they'd be stuck living in a place in which they felt unwanted.

Concurrently, *The San Francisco Chronicle* ran a seven-part series entitled, "Lethal Beauty," about suicides on the Golden Gate Bridge. Every night for a week, after my boys went to sleep, I'd read about all the distraught people who'd jumped from the span and died, or miraculously survived, mangled but alive. I was captivated by the stories of the families and friends the jumpers left behind, the CHP officers who were on the scene of the tragedy, the talkers who failed to negotiate the jumpers down, those who would later rummage through backpacks or purses to identify the bodies, the Coast Guard patrols who fished the bodies from the frigid bay.

Of everything I read, the following headline made the greatest impact: "Suicide by bridge is gruesome, and death is almost certain." I rolled my eyes. Wasn't that the point? But in reading the details of how the body falls at "roughly 75 to 80 miles per hour" and how you're screwed once your feet leave the bridge, I thought, That doesn't sound very pleasant.

To quote the series, "The force of the impact causes the internal organs to tear loose. Lacerated aortas, livers, spleens, and hearts. Broken ribs that may or may not be shoved into your heart or lungs. Skull fractures . . ." The list went on. If a jumper did die, versus landing himself in the hospital for weeks or months, it was either by asphyxiation or internal bleeding once he hit the cement-hard surface of the water.

Okay, so maybe I didn't really want to flail around in sixty-degree water until I drowned in my own blood. But what was an alternative? Most means of suicide are fairly gruesome, if not for me, then certainly for whoever would come across my corpse. Maybe it would be easier to go on living.

My current therapist urged me to see a psychiatrist. Desperate, I went in seeking anti-depressants and came out with a prescription for Lamictal, a drug to treat bi-polar disorder. In additional to being suicidal and severely depressed, I was now mildly bi-polar, mentally ill, chemically imbalanced—a familiar family label.

Even though I was frightened and ashamed by the tags, I somehow knew what the shrink said was true. I'd always dismissed my erratic behavior. I just enjoyed exceptionally high spirits and maybe sometimes acknowledged the whims of a quick temper, like kicking in the new kitchen cabinets after an argument with a friend. Admittedly, all those tantrums I threw as a kid—screaming and ripping apart fabric I'd incorrectly sewn together, pulling out handfuls of hair because the curls flipped the wrong way—fell far south of normal. And paranoia was one of the symptoms I could relate to. But mental illness, so rampant in my family, was a legacy I thought I'd outwitted.

While initially settling in with the idea that I was bi-polar, I feared no man would ever want to date me again. My *normal* friends would shun me. I'd end up being the reclusive, smelly cat-lady all the neighbors whispered about. Perhaps the most frustrating thing about being depressed is that all your thoughts fall into one of two categories: hopeless or more hopeless.

When my dosage of Lamictal reached fifty milligrams, my mood swings and depression began to lift. I started taking an interest in writing and gardening again. I laughed at the dinner table. My boys didn't appear as vigilant or nervous. I wasn't scared of having a panic attack or behaving irrationally in a crowded supermarket or in the cavernous parking lot of Barnes and Noble. The friends I had told about my new diagnosis didn't shun me as I'd feared. So I assured the psychiatrist that we didn't need to increase the dosage as planned. I was cured.

With the approach of the holiday season and the repeated misdiagnosis of another health issue, the suicidal thoughts returned. Apparently, they had just been taking a siesta. In a follow-up visit, my doctor decided to double my medication. At the next meeting, we added anti-depressants to the cocktail.

My sisters were incredibly supportive during this time: calling, emailing, sending me cards to say that they'd fly out in a jiffy if I needed help, that I better not do anything stupid or else *they'd* kill me. Slowly I felt a shift in my outlook. I no longer worried over every decision I made in a day. I realized my boys weren't the most unfortunate children on the planet just because they had two parents who couldn't be in the same room together. And I believed I wasn't the huge fuck-up I'd made myself out to be. I wasn't going to go broke tomorrow and find myself living on the street. The health issues I'd experienced recently were nothing compared to what many people faced every day.

Then something unbelievable happened. For the first time in my life I felt what it was like to have a *normal* response to an unpleasant event.

On Christmas Eve, I'd spent the afternoon writing and making a chicken gumbo for the next day. Just before I went to bathe for a party, I set a Tupperware container of the meal on the edge of the counter and opened the refrigerator. My elbow bumped the container and it tipped over. Warm soup splattered all over my pants, shoes, and the kitchen rug.

"Fuck," I said and stepped out of the brown puddle. In the past, I would have probably tried to pull the door off the refrigerator. At the very least, I would have stomped up and down, screaming and pounding my fists. I may have even, I'm ashamed to admit, thrown a plate at the cat when he came to see what all the fuss was about. But I simply stepped out of the mess and thought to myself, Thank God I dished the chicken up separately. Tomorrow I'll just make another roux with the extra vegetables and use canned broth. This is certainly inconvenient, but it's not the end of the world.

In the bathtub, I replayed these thoughts, compared them in my mind to how I would have reacted in the past, and it occurred to me that with an earlier diagnosis I could have been this person all along. The possibilities for my future felt so promising.

Since taking Lamictal and Prosac, my suicidal thoughts are largely gone. Of course, sometimes they stop by on occasion to see if I want to come out and play, to see if they can lure me onto the bridge. *After all, we're your loyal friends, your solace when everyone else lets you down.*

I've learned that if survival means taking anti-depressants and/or bi-polar medicine, then you pop the lid. Now I try not to see failed relationships, ill health, missed goals, career lows, and other disappointments as catastrophes. Sure, some events might not be what I had hoped for, but I can learn from all experience, grieve the losses, and move on.

A huge fear I had about taking medicine was that I'd then move through life numbed to both pleasure and pain. But that hasn't been the case. I still laugh with my sons. Creative projects still excite me to the point where I lay awake through the night playing with new ideas. I also feel disappointment and sadness. But the difference is that now these emotions don't control my life. Maybe that's the key: "If you can keep your head when all about you/Are losing theirs and blaming it on you . . . then you . . ." Just maybe, then you will live. Really live.

TAKING THE
LEAP

A T TIMES IN MY LIFE, I've sat on the sidelines and said to myself, "I wish I could do that." But fear often has the power to immobilize. Fear that an endeavor is too difficult, too expensive, too scary, too potentially humiliating dissuades even dipping a toe into the water. At thirty-six, I had nearly convinced myself I was simply too old and too busy as a single mom to take unnecessary risks. My time would be better spent focused on my children and earning a living. But all that changed one sunny spring day.

My sons, ages 3 and 5, were taking swim lessons at Sherman Swim School in Lafayette. While waiting for them, I watched the divers in the adjacent pool. There were two boards the kids practiced on. The taller board is approximately the same height as jumping off a single-story roof and the shorter one about the height of a kitchen table. Growing up in Louisiana, I had always loved to dive even though I had no formal training. Watching these divers now, I smiled at the fond memories of my eight siblings and me daring each other to try new "tricks" off our diving board, water slide, and platform trampoline. We were the neighborhood dare devils. But somewhere along my path from Mardi Gras queen to soccer mom that all changed. I'd bought into the stereotype that being a middle-aged mother meant acting like a grownup. And watching these kids perform on the boards filled me with envy and awe.

One afternoon I watched a man climb up the three-meter board. Prejudiced by his mid-section bulge and age (somewhere close to forty), I figured that from ten feet up in the air he'd do something simple like a swan dive. But when he flipped and twisted, I gasped. He toweled off and climbed back up to the ladder. I remembered, how in graduate school, I surprised my girlfriends with front and back somersaults off the one-meter at the Indian Valley JC pool. Then it occurred to me that if he could still dive, maybe I could as well.

I gathered my boys and approached Steve Sherman, the owner and head coach, about dive lessons. "They're not old enough," he said. "We recommend they start at age seven."

Embarrassed but determined, I explained that I was inquiring for myself. Steve blushed and introduced me to his father, Bob, who was sitting nearby on the bleachers. Bob told me he gave private lessons for beginners and, in fact, at seventy, he was still competing. I looked at this thin, but fit, wrinkled man and tried to picture my father with his bird legs and ample belly jumping from a three-meter board. But he was already dead, so no risk for him.

"You're quite the inspiration," I said and Bob smiled. Even now, nine years later, he is still setting world dive records.

I arrived at the first practice rattled with fear. I hoped I wouldn't make a fool of myself. Or get hurt. Did I really want to be seen in a bathing suit with stretch marks on my thighs and a horizontal bulge from my c-section? I kept tugging on my swimsuit, trying to cover as much of my body as possible. Should I tell the office that an emergency had arisen and I needed to cancel?

"Hey, Marie," Bob said as he came around the corner. "Ready to get started?"

I looked back at the entryway that led to the parking lot, to my car, to my quick departure. Marie, you can either lie and go home or show some bravery. Which will it be? You've paid for the lessons, hired a baby sitter. It's a beautiful day. You don't recognize any of the other parents here. Worst thing that could happen? The coward in me hissed: You could hit your head on the board, knock your teeth out, trash the last of your good looks. A tug of war ensued until I finally decided to step up.

Springboards are much springier than they appear. On your first try you're likely to find yourself flying across the pool, hoping gravity sets in before you take a bite out of the cement.

On my first jump, I soared like Wonder Woman. All speed, no grace. Ever hit the surface of the water with your face? It feels a lot like, I'd imagine, stepping in the direct line of a firefighter's hose on full blast. The wallop can cause bruises.

On my second attempt, as Bob suggested, I tightened the fulcrum to create more tension, less springiness. "Just bounce a few times on the end of the board to get your balance," he said. Circling my arms like a penguin trying to lift off, I was thankful that without my glasses I couldn't see whether any of the other parents were amusing themselves at the sight of my uncoordinated flab jiggling on the board. Finally, when I managed to bounce a half dozen times without falling into the water, I tried another front jump. This time, I didn't smack my face.

Despite the first few welts to both pride and body, I soon quit worrying about appearances. I simply worked hard at improving my balance and form, and I actually began to enjoy myself. Three times a week, Bob greeted me at the pool with a hug. He referred to me as his star pupil, meaning whatever new dive he'd ask me to tackle, I'd try. Sometimes I met new challenges with success, other times not. The bruises on my arms and legs were badges of courage.

Many of my friends were surprised by my newfound passion and apparent athleticism. Several had only known me as an overweight mom who occasionally hiked the foothills of Mt. Diablo. But not all my family and friends were supportive. There were the naysayers, the ones who focused on the potential dangers and humiliation. "How will you care for your sons when you're fully paralyzed? Don't you feel ridiculous at your age?" Rather than dissuade me, their skepticism empowered me to prove them wrong. Taking these risks on the boards, overcoming my fears, made me feel more alive than I had in years. The body I had hidden under baggy clothes was growing firmer and more capable.

By mid-summer, I'd taken two series of lessons and learned the basic dives required to join the team. Working out in groups of six or seven was a lot of cheaper than taking private lessons. The first afternoon as a new member of Sherman Divers, I approached the trampoline and Steve introduced me to my teammates. A half dozen children, ages seven to seventeen, looked at me as a curiosity at best, though more likely, an intruder. I remembered from my own childhood that parents were better not seen or heard unless from behind the wheel of the car or pulling out the credit card. I worried I might impede these kids' progress.

To give the children the space I felt I'd want if the situation were reversed, I usually swam laps between turns or sat on the bench next to Steve. But it wasn't long before they pulled me into their conversations and quarrels, and I felt like one of the group. Some of the younger girls would swim over between dives and cling to my arms like my sons did when they were small. Initially I was uncomfortable with their affections. I'd never been touchy-feely. But gradually I accepted their hugs as harmless, even sweet, and I no longer pulled away. It was so cute to hear their squeaky voices saying, "Come on, Marie, you can do it!" And it felt strange to find myself struggling with the same dive as a person three decades my junior.

Over the next four years, I participated in local NORCAL meets against other divers of varying abilities. Within this tight-knit group some divers were quite competitive, some were experienced (either from diving in college or coaching at the high school level), and some had their own facilities in which to practice. And on the periphery there were the few newcomers like me.

In 2002, Bob finally talked me and another diver from our team into signing up for a National Masters Dive Competition in Dallas. He said one of the benefits of larger meets was that you learned how to perform under pressure. "Besides," he added, "only two women in your age group showed up at Nationals last year, which means, at the very least, you'd take third place and get a medal. And they give out some really nice medals." He made a circle with his hands to indicate the size. I laughed. At forty, I might not have too many more opportunities for such glory.

Despite Bob's assurances, seven women in the 40 - 44 age

category registered. At the introductory meeting, I learned some of my competitors still performed in exhibitions and most of them actively coached. Carla, the strongest and most favored among the divers, was a near certainty for first place. The Wrigley Twins, as I'd privately named two blond women wearing similar neon Speedos, would vie for second. And there were other serious contenders as well. So much for third place.

Throughout the warm-up for the three-meter event, my nerves were jumping. Not since those first private lessons had ten feet from the edge of a board to the surface of the water seemed so far up. An endless loop of self-defeating thoughts played in my head.

As the event's line up was announced, judges assembled on deck with their plastic score cards. I started off with a simple front dive straight. It hadn't nearly the finesse of Carla's or The Twins' but it was respectable. On the next round, the announcer called, "Etienne. 201C. Back dive tuck."

I climbed the ladder. Adjusted the fulcrum. Drew in a huge breath. This dive was tricky for me. It required balance and confidence, both of which were in short supply that day. Usually, in local meets, by late afternoon when the master divers' events finally began, the stands had nearly emptied. But that wasn't the case now. The deck teemed with activity. The stands were filled with spectators. From below, Bob yelled, "Here you go, Marie." I nodded and walked to the edge, turned carefully, and inched my way backward until my feet were half on and half off the board. I tried to picture the dive that the six judges were waiting to see but my mind went completely blank. I'd just done three of these in practice but now couldn't see anything but the bright, white sunshine. My legs shook. I could feel myself tipping backward. With outstretched arms, I tried to recover my balance but it was like an invisible hand had reached out and tapped my shoulder. Good-bye! My knees collapsed and I fell. My feet loudly slapped the water as they hit first.

"Failed dive," the announcer said. "Zero."

Fighting back tears, I climbed out of the pool and avoided eye contact with Bob. As I dried off, one of the Wrigley Twins strolled over in her neon suit. She set her hands on her hips and said, "Are you going back up again? You don't look very confident."

I shrugged her off and made my way to the bathroom, where I let all my negativity unravel: You're just fooling yourself, Marie. You're no diver. You're a divorced mom who dons a bathing suit twice a week to flip and twist in the air like a twelve-year-old. "Master" diver, my fat ass.

Then I thought—Stop that!—and splashed water on my face. One failed dive. So what? Get back on the board. Show that chewing-gum twit and everyone else that you're no quitter. To hell with the medal. Get out there and have some fun.

I took last place in Dallas, but I didn't quit. The next year at Nationals in Hawaii I upped the ante with new dives of higher degrees of difficulty and took last again. At least I was consistent!

•••

L ATELY, ONE OF THE SCARIEST dives I have been working on is a back-one-and-a-half-somersault. The first time I stood on the three-meter board, the glassy surface of the water glistening ominously below, I tried to summon the courage but my legs trembled. Concentrate, Marie. You can do this. I yelled down to Steve, "Call me out. Be prepared for anything."

He held a megaphone to his mouth and talked to me like he did with the kids: "Got you. I'll do the hard work. You just come out on my call."

I tried to visualize the perfect dive, but I couldn't sense the rhythm. In each imagined trial, I let go of my legs too early and landed flat on my back. I shook away this image and asked a fellow diver on deck to turn on the bubble machine. An eight foot circle of bubbles would lessen the impact should I land on my back.

"Just get off the board. Your body will know what to do," Steve called. The bleachers were half-filled with parents and divers. My worst fear was landing the wrong way and breaking my neck. "Don't think about it anymore. You're ready."

With my arms stretched above my head, I focused straight ahead on the tree tops and began priming the board, moving rhythmically up and down as I counted one, two, three, and four . . . Circling my arms with one final, deep depression, I lifted off. My legs came up into a tuck, my knees to my chest, and I held on tight, spinning backward. I'm doing it. I'm doing it, I thought. Then panic set in. Has Steve forgotten to call me out? Should I let go now? Oh God, this is going to hurt.

When I finally heard him yell, "Hup!" I kicked my feet toward the sky, looked back at the water, and reached hard. My hands broke through the bubbles first and I felt an immense relief as the rest of my body painlessly followed. When I resurfaced, I grinned. Steve, my fellow divers, and the other parents were applauding.

"I did it!" I yelled. "I did it!"

"Good job. Now do another one just like that but this time bring it in to first base. And keep your legs together." He pointed to his flip-flop that he'd set four feet from the edge of the board to indicate first base. Unlike baseball (or sex), landing anywhere past first base was unacceptable. Balance, finesse, and a splashless entry were the three keys of a high-scoring dive. For Steve, it was not enough to simply execute the dive. He wanted it closer to the board, on first base, and no sunlight between the ankles. I laughed and couldn't wait to get back up on the board.

In August 2006, Stanford University hosted the XI FINA World Masters Championships. The good news was about half the regulars from the U.S. had aged out of my category. However, women from regions worldwide had replaced them. Knowing I faced stiff competition, my goal was simply to throw some new dives and perform to the best of my ability, even if that meant coming in last yet again.

During warm-ups for the first event, I smacked my face several times while trying to ignore my sons' constant ridicule from the deck area. Austin kept taking pictures of me, and between every dive, he'd shove the digital camera in my face while he and his brother laughed at me. I had insisted they attend one of my events because I wanted them to see how their mom had improved and to see some world-class divers compete, especially the men in the under-forty groups. After hearing Steve say over and over, "Concentrate, Marie. Pretend this is just like any other day," I finally told my sons if they weren't going to be supportive, they could find some other place to situate themselves.

Once they were out of sight, I regained my composure. Out of fourteen women in my group, I placed eighth on the one-meter and eleventh on the three-meter—my best showing ever.

On the drive back to Walnut Creek, my sons said that placing eighth and eleventh was nothing to be proud of. I didn't even earn a medal. I wanted to say, "Look here, you little brats! Let's see you do better." Instead, I said, "That is so unkind. At least I showed up and tried. I didn't let fear get in my way. There may be thousands of women around the world who on any given day can throw a better back-one-and-a-half-with-a-half-twist than me, but they weren't here today. Of the women who did show up, I scored somewhere in the middle of the group. I'm proud of my performance. I got out there and did my best." I wanted to add, "So there, you little losers," but I thought of my mother and restrained myself.

TAKE ME TO THE
MARDI GRAS

MY FRIEND CATHY AND I were having tea in my bedroom since our four rowdy boys had overtaken the other end of the house with their disturbing, M-rated video games.

"Someone mentioned they were at your house for a party and saw your queen's costume," Cathy said. She touched the gold-beaded fringed sleeves of the Mardi Gras gown that hung on a headless mannequin next to my bed. "They said it was odd you still displayed it, like you were stuck in the past. Thought perhaps it was time for you to move on with your life."

I knew immediately who she was talking about: my jerk of an ex-boyfriend who always had to have the final word. "I'll take that under advisement," I said and then I switched subjects. As we began trading stories about our week, I picked a few hair balls out of the elaborate beadwork and made a note to ask my housekeeper to shoo away Toby and Shelby, my cats, if she caught them playing under the skirt. Their games of chase plus my twenty years of moving the dress to and fro had worked loose patches of beads and rhinestones.

After Cathy left, I climbed back into bed with my newspaper. The cats, as they always did at the end of a night, tore down the hall past Austin and Zack's rooms, leaped onto my mattress to alternately bite, lick, and wrestle each other, then when Toby got too aggressive, Shelby hissed, jumped off, and darted under the Mardi Gras dress with Toby right on her tail. The headless dress swayed back and forth.

"Out of there, you dumb cats," I yelled and clapped my hands. "Vamoose!"

They ignored me, as they were prone to do. I grabbed a paperback off the headboard behind me and threw the book at the dress. It dipped toward the window and gold beads broke loose. At the sound of the beads hitting the hardwood and rolling across the floor, Toby's orange-striped head poked out. He and his gray-striped sister batted the tiny gold balls until they lost them under the bureau and loveseat.

With the cats now settled at my side and grooming each other, I looked at the costume from my reign as Queen Berengaria of Navarre of 1983—the loose threads, the cracked beads, the missing rhinestones, the dented collar—and I remembered my disappointment at seeing its poor condition when I'd first unpacked it a decade after bringing it with me from Louisiana. From one apartment to the next, it had been crammed in a box. To my dismay, moisture had darkened the beige fabric as well as loosened the beadwork. Rather than stuff it back into a box, I had decided to display it, thinking that might help preserve it. Maybe someday Austin and Zack would want to show it off to a girlfriend and say, "My mom was the queen of a ball. Isn't her dress awesome?"

Cathy's comments stung. Was I really stuck in the past? Perhaps she and this ex-boyfriend had expressed what many also thought. But I loved my dress. I loved all the happy memories associated with it. At one time, the gown my friend mocked draped a body slim and young. At each fitting, I traded the reality of my life for the safety of fantasy. I was a fucking queen for a year.

This wasn't a gown you'd find at Macy's. It was a one-of-a-kind work of art that cost my father thousands of dollars. Two dressmakers spent a full year designing, sewing, and decorating it.

Many of my California friends had been curious about these balls they'd only read about in books and newspapers. "What was it like," they'd often asked, "the whole Mardi Gras experience?" I'd tell them it was sort of like getting married: Your photograph and an official announcement appeared in the newspaper; you registered for silver goblets at a local boutique; gifts and flowers were delivered daily to your door with congratulatory notes from Krewe members and family friends; you were chauffeured to parties and luncheons where you were the guest of honor; there were receiving lines, fittings, more fittings, another picture in the paper in your full costume; there was the Friday night rehearsal ball to which you'd invite your second-tier friends; there was a lot of hurry up and wait and short tempers; and finally, on Saturday night, you get to enjoy "The Ball." For a few exciting, scary, surreal hours you would be the Belle of the Ball. Then the very next day you'd go back to being just another college kid . . . with a really cool dress.

I was a junior in college when I was chosen as the 31st Queen of the Troubadours. Most girls reigned in their teens.

The year before, my younger sister had played the role of Lady Edith, Her Royal Highness. I had sat with my family in the audience and watched my sister curtsey from one corner of the stage to another in her stunning pink dress, a twenty-eight piece orchestra and chorus providing the background music. My sister was a tomboy and only agreed to participate in the ball because it made Daddy so proud. Watching her wave at the cheering crowd, I was filled with envy. And as was my custom to talk to God only when I desperately wanted a favor, I begged him to let me be Queen next year. I was surprised when I received the nomination, especially after a few falling-down drunk performances at prior balls. But you can't fight divine intervention.

Now some people will say Mardi Gras balls are ridiculous, pompous spectacles that perpetuate the fantasies of middle-aged men and post-pubescent princesses. And having finally witnessed one sober in 2000 with my sons, I must admit the sight of local businessmen, doctors, and lawyers goose-stepping around a stage in satin capes, ruffles, short sequined dresses, and stockings is rather silly. But if you can suspend all judgment and just allow yourself to enjoy the pageantry, the evening can be great fun.

All it takes is a glance at a Gras Ball program to see that the participants are not chosen for their beauty alone. It's really a bit of a popularity contest, related specifically to how well the Director of a particular Krewe gets along with the royalty's parents. Other adults, in general, found Daddy and Momma were easy to work with. Just as they never showed up at our schools making demands, they never asked for special favors or tried to exert any influence on how things were done. They merely paid their dues and made sure we arrived on time.

Worse than troublesome parents, it seemed, was a girl who gained weight and couldn't fit into her costume. Once the final measurements were noted in the designers' notebooks, and the fabric was cut, it was almost a mortal sin to pork out until your reign was complete. Smelling salts were kept on hand to accommodate those who starved themselves days before the photo shoot and fainted in the hot afternoon sun. I remember well the Director grumbling about one prominent family whose daughter had weight problems. She shook her head and complained just above a whisper how so-and-so needed to have another panel sewn into her dress. I made sure this never happened to me.

Since the Mardi Gras balls were intended to be a family affair, the girls weren't meant to look like the cast from "Dangerous Liaisons," with heaving bosoms bursting from their bodices. But I do remember the dressmaker tugging and pulling on my gown, deliberating whether or not to lower the neckline a couple more inches. I thought, Yes, yes, please . . . I want to show more cleavage. But God had other plans.

For days after Cathy's comment, I felt ashamed. Was I really stuck in the past? When I began writing about my childhood and our family, stories that would be incorporated into *Storkbites*, some of my sisters often accused me of this, i.e., no forward movement. They'd say, "You're such a kid, you'll never grown up. . . ." Maybe they were right.

THE GINGERBREAD
HOUSE

HEADING OUT FOR A WEEKEND with their father, Austin and Zack stopped at the kitchen table where I was working on this year's gingerbread house. For the framework, I'd constructed a two-story structure out of architecture foam board. The design was loosely based on one of Thomas Kincaid's paintings of a quaint cottage. Only my version was on steroids.

"Mom, when are you going to give up?" Zack said. "It looks terrible."

He was right. The frosting was too thin, the candy kept sliding down the glossy walls, and the gingerbread cookies I'd baked to approximate a stone façade looked, as Austin so kindly noted, like what we scooped daily out of our cat's litter box. But I was no quitter. Besides, even though I was getting frustrated by the project, I had faith it would turn out okay. I wasn't wasting my time and money, as the kids said. I was giving myself the gift of an all-engrossing, fun, creative activity.

"Run along," I said, "if you can't be more supportive."

One thing I've learned about making gingerbread houses is that often more is more. If it looks like a bayou shack, just keep adding more candy and frosting until it's as elegant as a New Orleans Victorian lady on St. Charles Avenue.

On Monday, I proudly unveiled my masterpiece. "Wow! How'd you do that?" Zack exclaimed.

"I didn't give up."

The boys walked around the house checking out every detail. Their fingers traced the sprawling ivy that climbed up walls, the yellow stained-glass of the windows made of butter-scotch, the candy-covered chimney where Santa was perched. "By the way, avoid nibbling on the stone walls. I used black ink in the frosting for the mortar. Might be toxic." At two-thirty Sunday morning, I'd run out of energy and options.

My fascination with building gingerbread houses began two decades ago when I was 23 and still living in Louisiana. Upon earning a B.S. in Business Administration in 1985, I received a passbook containing the annual dividends from my share of stock in our family business that my father had saved for me. With more than $20,000, I now had the means to realize a life-long dream: to head out west and begin afresh. But before I did, I wanted to make handmade holiday gifts for my family and friends. Even though I could now buy extravagant presents, I felt something homemade would mean more to them.

For two of my sisters, I made cotton nightgowns with lacy collars. I created a handbag for a special friend, scented can-dles for others. My parents were more difficult. There wasn't much they couldn't buy for themselves, and their interests outside the house had greatly waned.

On Christmas Eve, I still hadn't the foggiest notion of what to make for my parents. Time was running out. I looked at my watch and thought, I can still hit the mall before it closes. I grabbed my purse when an idea struck. Why not make a gingerbread house? A one of a kind creation, something they couldn't find in a catalog?

My father always loved the trimmings and fanfare of the holidays. He'd hang swags of plastic owl globes on the eves of the front porch and tuck blinking lights in the shrubs. He'd bring home a huge, fragrant tree that my siblings and I would cover with tacky ornaments and tinsel. He'd write out checks and order rhinestone brooches for my mother to tuck with other gifts inside eleven furry red-white stockings, tied to the banister with velvet ribbon. He'd buy spiced nuts, red pistachios, and fruitcake that was actually eaten. And every holiday, he'd order a gingerbread house for our dining room table. My brothers, sisters, and I were forbidden to nibble or touch it until Christmas night when it would be ours to devour.

I headed to the grocery store and realized when I got to the baking aisle that I didn't know what I was doing. So I did what I always do in a panic—buy a lot of everything.

That evening, two of my sisters gathered in my kitchen to watch the construction. I used square cake pans and soon pulled two warm spice cakes from my oven. I cut them up, stacked the layers, figured I'd just use a can of white frosting to hold the pieces together and approximate the shape of a little cottage.

An hour into the enterprise, one of my sisters shook her head and suggested I find a late-night drug store to buy a something "not so ugly." Ignoring her skepticism, I tried to fortify the lopsided, lumpy mess with a box of assorted toothpicks. My sisters snickered when the dye from the toothpicks discolored the frosting.

"Leave! Both of you. Now!"

Free from their sneers, I studied the mess and fought off tears. Bowls of candies, pretzels, and frosting baited me from the counter, waiting to be put to good use. I considered, for an instant, tossing the heap into the garbage.

"Structure. Stability. That's what it needs," I told myself. I rummaged through my townhouse, searching for something, I didn't know what. My grandmother's antique secretary caught my eyes. I found a drawing tablet and tore off the cardboard covers. With a ruler, a pencil, tape, and scissors, I constructed a sturdy frame and crammed the demolished cake into its hollow interior.

Who'll know the difference? I thought, feeling my tension ease. As Barbra Streisand belted out Christmas carols on the living room stereo, I covered the exterior with graham crackers. Overlapping rows of thin wheat crackers transformed into a shake roof. Once I had created a structurally sound base, I added windows, a door, a pebble walkway, strings of lights, and shrubs from the jelly beans, gumdrops, licorice, Lifesavers, M & Ms, and pretzels. Christmas morning, I placed the gingerbread house before my parents. Daddy grinned so wide I could see the fillings in his molars. Even my mother seemed impressed.

"You bought it," one of my sisters said and punched my arm. "No way that's the thing you were working on last night."

My brothers and sisters circled around the coffee table, and I smiled at the attention my masterpiece received. I never told anyone what lay inside those graham cracker walls, mashed up cake, and fifty plus toothpicks bleeding blue, green, red, and yellow into lumpy frosting. Daddy must have loved my gift. He forbade anyone to pinch even a gumdrop. After the holidays he shellacked it for display all year round. It wasn't until nearly a decade later, when my parents downsized, that my creation made its way to the garbage can.

Several holidays passed before I built another gingerbread house. As a new mom, I wanted to create my own family traditions. From architecture foam board, a cement-like white frosting, graham crackers, and gobs of candy emerged my second masterpiece. I added coconut flakes to give the yard that just-snowed Tahoe appearance.

When Austin and Zack entered preschool, the tradition grew to include our friends. I'd start in November, building frames for twenty or more houses out of milk cartons or cardboard. Pretty soon, every surface in my kitchen would be covered in houses. Then we'd invite parents and their children over for a decorating party. The children's eyes would glaze over when they spotted the bowls of licorice, peppermints, gummy bears, cookies, and jelly beans. Gobbling down ten pieces of candy for every one they applied seemed the agreed-upon ratio. When the sugar catapulted into the children's bloodstream, they'd bolt from the table, passing off the project to mom or dad, then run outside to play. It was fun to watch the parents take ownership of these often haphazardly-decorated houses and see their enthusiasm build as they transformed the messes into masterpieces.

We'd borrow each other's ideas and help trouble-shoot a roof that refused to stay put. Not only did we create a village of candy-coated houses, we created fond memories of laughter and awe. As our friends carefully carried their creations to their cars, they thanked me profusely for opening my home to such chaos. Season and after season, this was a special gift I gave to my sons, friends, and myself.

One year, before kits became widely available from retailers, I found a way of sharing my love of decorating houses with my sisters and their families who lived in Louisiana. I prepared all-in-one packages: the house form, frosting ingredients, instructions, and enough decorating supplies to cover the walls, roof, and snow-covered lawns. Weeks later, photos from my sisters arrived. My sons and I studied the details, lifting ideas for the following year.

Even though all our lives are so hectic, I still get such joy from giving handmade gifts, something that says, "This was made just for you. Please accept my time and love." A gift doesn't have to cost a lot to mean plenty.

THE CYCLE OF
ABUSE

IT TOOK YEARS OF THERAPY FOR ME to realize there is no getting around self-control. Season after season, I'd sit in my therapist's loft office and confess my latest outburst. I'd describe how a simple argument over whether or not one son could skip a Little League baseball game would escalate into me screaming, pounding on his door, threatening him with a loss of privileges, and pleading for him to put on his uniform until we'd both be in tears while my other son cowered in his bedroom.

Through rain, hail, and blazing sunshine, I'd sit on the sofa across from my therapist and look at the impatience, disappointment, and worry on her face. I'd describe the overwhelming feelings I'd carry with me for days after each fit.

Shame: Is there any wonder my sons flinch when I come near them, even in apology, after a tantrum? What would my friends and my sons' teachers think if they knew I wasn't as sweet as I behaved in public?

Hopelessness: Will my sons grow up to hate me? Will *I'm sorry* be hollow, meaningless words to them?

Anger: Why can't they just behave so I don't have to get so angry? Why did my parents have children if they were only going to abuse us and leave behind a legacy of monsters?

Fear: What if my ex-husband or therapist contacts Child Protective Services to take my sons away? What if other parents come to my door unexpectedly and hear my fits? What if they won't allow their children to play with mine anymore?

I was a stay-at-home, divorced mom for most of my boys' lives. At times, I didn't handle the stress of this job very gracefully even though I was fortunate enough to afford quality domestic help and child care. If there had been one of those nanny cameras in my house, surely CPS would have been knocking at my door. Not often, a half dozen times in total, I lost my wits and got physical. It was simple action-reaction, a behavior I'd learned at a very early age.

Once, I was struggling to restrain Zack while diapering him. Wanting to be free to resume play with Austin, he grabbed a metal toy and whacked me on the head. Without a second thought, I turned him over onto his belly and began spanking his bare bottom with a vengeance. He wailed. As my hand came down one final time, I saw the hypocrisy of my reaction: hitting him for hitting me. As for Austin, I spanked him five times in his early years. The last instance left my handprint on his back. After that, I told myself that under no circumstances would I ever physically harm either of my boys again. And I haven't.

Even though I was able to stop the physical abuse with my sons, I've had a more difficult time controlling my emotional and verbal attacks. Some days, my tirades weren't really directed at my own children, who were merely convenient targets. Arguments with friends, my ex-husband, or my sisters, perceived injustices or slights would all end with me kicking in cabinet doors, breaking furniture, or screaming at my sons for some minor infraction until my throat was raw.

I used to yell and break Austin and Zack's toys in fits of frustration. Say friends were coming to dinner and just before their arrival I was frantically running through the house trying to clean up all the toys and dirty clothes. My mind would race with worry: What would our guests think if they saw how messy we actually were? Would they not like me anymore? Instead of enlisting the boys' help, or training them to put their things away, or even telling myself not to stress over what my friends thought, I'd curse everyone under my breath. One stubbed toe was all it took to catapult me into a fit of rage. I'd holler and hurl the offending toy—a Brio train, a Power Ranger, a Duplo block—across the room. Then I'd scream. Times like this would cause Austin to ask, "Mommy, why are you so nice to strangers and so mean at home?" This was when my hopelessness led to suicidal daydreams. Without me, the boys would be spared such misery.

In therapy for years, I analyzed my verbal abusiveness in an attempt to understand it. What really prompted me to act this way? Why couldn't I stop myself when the rage welled up inside? I believed that if I could understand my tantrums and anticipate them, then perhaps I could avoid them in the future. I looked at my behavior from an intellectual stance. Surely there was some key to unlocking the inner workings of my mind, to rewiring my brain. Was it a resentment of my sons' innocence, as someone once suggested? Their audacity in refusing to cooperate with me? I would have never been so bold as to openly defy my mother.

I tried to identify the full extent of my own abuse and neglect. To tame the monster inside me, I unearthed every hurt I'd suffered, every wrong that had nourished this beast into being. Through my writing and therapy, and with friends, family, and support groups, I expressed my long-suppressed anger. I grieved the losses of my innocence as a young child and a promiscuous teen. I grieved over the sudden deaths of my brothers, parents, and grandparents. Yet I felt totally disconnected from who I wanted to be, who I thought I was, who I knew I could be.

Since I didn't have positive role models as parents and felt insecure about my own abilities, I sought guidance elsewhere. I observed other parents at parks, at school, in department stores, at sporting events, Cub Scouts, parties, new parent and child support/play groups to see how the moms and dads handled conflict, set boundaries. While I tried to emulate good parenting—the approaches that seemed to have the most positive results—I'd continue to put myself down: Why can't I do that? Why must I fly into a rage when things don't go my way? Surely their childhood wasn't perfect yet they aren't terrorizing their children.

Eventually I gathered the courage, swallowed my pride, and risked exposure by admitting my struggles. I talked to my boys' teachers, their pediatrician, our friends, and my sisters. This was a time of trial and error. See what works and what doesn't, then go from there.

"What's your secret?" I'd ask. "Don't you just want to wring their necks sometimes? Or scream until they finally do what you want?"

"Sure," a parent or teacher might say. "My patience has limits just like everyone else's. But I'll ask myself, 'Is this battle worth me getting so upset? Is it really the end of the world if they don't make one swim meet? Or if their room isn't immaculate? Or if they forget their homework?'"

But it seemed so easy for them. They had husbands, wives, partners, family . . . close by. They had confidence, patience, training. They were better than I was.

"What's the secret?" I once asked an older friend who admitted to having a temper. He'd confided that in the past he'd also punched holes in doors, left the house in a fury after arguments, screamed at his kids till they shook with terror.

"There is no secret," he said. "Just got to decide from here on you won't lash out at your kids. No ifs, ands, or buts. It's all about self-control. Like you do with your friends. When was the last time you got angry and threw a broken hammer at a girlfriend or called her names until she left your house crying?"

What he said made sense. But his answer still seemed too vague to take hold of. I needed step by step instructions that I could follow like a recipe.

One day, the conversation came up again. This time he said, "Empathy. Yes, empathy. Perhaps that's what it was. Recognizing the terror from my own childhood in my daughter's eyes. Knowing the fear and hurt she was feeling as I railed at her."

This was good. But still not a surefire strategy. I investigated the wealth of information available to struggling parents in classes and lectures at the children's schools and adult ed, in newspaper and magazine advice columns, parenting books, the Internet. Many of these resources allowed me to remain anonymous and therefore I was less afraid than if I were to go to the library and say, "Where are your books on child abuse? I'm about to go ballistic and I need some preventative advice."

I sought the advice of some of my sisters who I figured would be supportive rather than judgmental. One offered a very helpful idea. She'd heard the acronym HALT (Hungry, Angry, Lonely, and Tired), which was used in AA meetings, and suggested that I try to preempt my outbursts by recognizing when I'm most at risk of behaving inappropriately, when I'm in a less than optimal emotional or physical state. When hungry, angry, lonely, or tired, I should avoid stressful situations, projects, or activities. For instance, hanging Christmas lights (*ugh*) or assembling bookshelves (*bigger ugh*). I now try to pick a time when I'm rested and well fed. I will ask myself: Does this task need to be done today? Can it wait until another adult is available to help or watch the kids? Does it really need to be perfect? I might decide to wait until my boys are at their dad's house to tackle jobs that make me want to put the hammer through the door. That way, if things go awry, at least my boys won't be home to witness my wrath. And often, I can just hire a handyman instead of killing myself (and those around me).

HALT reminds me of the warning that came with my power saw: "Exercise extreme caution. Don't use this tool if you are tired, angry, or have insufficient time to finish the job."

Look around at shopping malls, airports, and even theme parks, and you'll see many tired, angry, hungry parents who've pushed themselves and their kids too far. Constant threats of "Stop that or I'll spank you" blend right in with "It's a small world after all . . ." It's taken me a long time to learn to set limits with my boys, to say no without feeling guilty, to set boundaries that help me remain sane, to take care of myself.

I'm a huge advocate of setting aside time for just me. I find that when I'm physically, mentally, and spiritually fit

I'm better able to care for my children. Loving myself and honoring my needs sets a good example for my sons. My joint custody arrangement with my ex-husband affords me considerable free time to recharge my batteries. But for single parents or parents who are often the primary caregivers, my advice would be to hire a sitter, join a babysitting co-op, trade off with your partner or another parent to give yourself an afternoon or evening off. Find a hobby. Take a walk. A friend of mine with three young children couldn't afford a sitter. So when her husband came home at night, she let him put the children to bed and spent an hour at Long's Drugs filling and then emptying a shopping cart. While this might sound totally crazy, it didn't cost her a penny, and it preserved her sanity.

As my sons have grown older, my confidence as a parent has increased. I've put together a tool chest of strategies that work for us. And as they enter their teen years, we are able to work together on more complicated projects. They can help me navigate the London underground, trouble-shoot my computer, decipher a knotty French phrase. Now that the whole burden doesn't lie on my shoulders, I feel safer, grounded, better equipped to take on new challenges. As a result, my outbursts are less frequent and I've slowly begun to gain control of my temper.

Luckily, I stopped drinking shortly before I married and had children. If I was still getting blitzed three or four nights a week, my children would suffer greatly.

In the end, it all comes down to self-control—behaving like an adult, doing the right thing, loving your children more than your anger. I know now that I can't blame my eruptions on my sons' misbehavior, on circumstances, or on my own childhood abuse. Yelling, throwing tantrums, spanking: these last resorts don't work. Violence begets violence.

I won't lie and say I'm completely cured. In July 2006, I went ballistic because Austin hated his new haircut so much he wouldn't get out of the car and go to his pottery class. I pleaded, bribed, demanded, and finally resorted to name calling and yelling until he was in tears. His brother was in the car as well, terrified, chewing on his nails. All of us now have to live with this experience for the rest of our lives. And for what? A stupid pottery class? It seemed so important to me at the time because if my son didn't go, he'd fall behind and not be able to keep up with his peers. But a pottery class?

So after hearing his own mother say some terribly cruel things he will remember for the rest of his life, Austin still refused to go to the class, while I ended up with a sore throat and a heart full of shame and regret. I could never take back what I said or its implications. Just as my father could never take back the shame and hurt he inflicted on the car trip so long ago when he yelled at me for picking mayonnaise out of my sandwich with a toothpick. Just as my drunken mother could never take back her spoken wish that my brother was dead. And the next day he was.

But for each failure, there have been dozens more successes. I've tried to create a home environment that lends itself to harmony. When my boys demonstrate kindness toward each other, I try to recognize it and say how proud I am of them. If they shoot their air-soft guns at the furniture, which is explicitly against house rules, the guns are tossed in the garbage permanently. Rather than tell them ten times to brush their teeth then rage when they ignore me, I will say, "It's time to brush," and walk them to the bathroom. Eventually, they will learn without me standing guard at the door. This approach requires more work up front, but the payoff is that I don't let the simple tasks build to an all-out war. And in the end, I'm helping all of us develop quality life skills.

THE BEAUTY
OF BEING

I HAVE FOUND MYSELF, to varying degrees, envious of others because they are thinner or taller, wealthier, smarter, more popular, more successful, or more creative. I've envied those with firmer bodies, fewer wrinkles, perfect skin, white teeth, loving parents, exotic eyes, lots of children, stronger legs, quicker speed, more patience, thicker hair, longer nails, slender fingers, and perfectly manicured toes. I've envied some because they are better writers or musically inclined, because they have partners or spouses they adore, or because they have better parenting skills.

One afternoon on my way to the Rossmoor Safeway—the old folks' store, my sons would complain, for its annoyingly slow clientele—I took a detour into the Rossmoor Beauty Salon I'd ignored for years. A few days earlier, I'd asked Austin to trim my hair. I wanted a simple, straight cut. Only problem was that it was now lopsided. With each hurried snip, each clump of chlorine and sun-bleached blond hair that fell to the tile floor, I knew it wouldn't be even. But he seemed so pleased with himself I waited until he'd left the bathroom to make a few adjustments on my own, which still didn't do the trick. Before Prosac and Lamictal, I might have had a meltdown over my *ruined* hair, pulling it out in clumps, throwing the comb at the mirror, kicking at the cabinets. But now, I rationalized, I'd known the risks when I handed him the scissors. There was no State Cosmetology Certification hanging over his bathroom mirror. And the beautiful thing about hair is that it grows back.

From the door of the salon I could smell the perm solution, hairspray, and a slight trace of sour milk, which reminded me of my clothes when I was nursing my sons. This no-frills place was just the sort of beauty parlor my mother would have gone to for her weekly wash, set, and dry. A couple of silver-haired women waited in the lobby. About half the stations in back were filled with customers. The hairstylists and I were the only women in the shop younger than sixty.

Heads slowly turned my way as I added my name to the waiting list then sat in one of the chairs facing the front windows. I checked my watch, 1:15 p.m., and wondered how long it would be before my name was called. I needed to pick up my sons by 3 p.m. A young African-American woman wheeled an old man up the sidewalk. They stopped in front of the shop. She reached for the handle and I quickly sprung from my chair.

"Thank you," she said as I held open the door. The man gave me a half nod from the corner of the salon in which he was parked. His caregiver went to the cash register and wrote his name on the list. Discreetly, I studied the man and his wheelchair. He had an oxygen tank, its plastic tubing attached to his nostrils. I wondered if this was his big outing for the day.

Soon, a short bus pulled up to the curb. Several residents

from the Rossmoor Retirement Community descended and slowly disbursed. Two women helped each other to the salon door, huge grandma handbags hanging from the crook of their elbows. I got up, and once again, held open the door. The chairs in the lobby filled. Another woman came pushing her walker toward the salon. Looking at the faded yellow tennis balls affixed to the base of her walker, I smiled and rose to help her. At my last accounting job, when I mentioned I played tennis, my co-worker asked that I bring my dead balls to the office so she could give them to her grandmother. The loose flap of skin under the woman's chin jiggled as she crept by me. I could see the bulky outline of her Depends and thought, This could be me in thirty years.

"Please have my seat," I said and removed my purse. Standing off to the side, I looked around the salon. These old people had the wherewithal to drag their tired bones out of bed to get spruced up. And for what? A trip to the cafeteria or bingo room later that evening? A visit to their internist? Behind all the wrinkles, liver spots, bald heads, cancer scars, saggy flesh, and all the other nicks and scars were stories, memories, losses, and with any luck still some hopes and dreams. There was something very sad and beautiful about these old people. On one hand they seemed so vulnerable, utterly dependent on others, yet they also appeared to have accepted their limitations. They were at a point in their lives where death was irrefutable. And envy, or being discontent with their lot, was silly. It occurred to me that it's less frustrating to make the best of your situation, no matter what it is, than to fight it. Maybe acceptance is going about your business and finding that no matter where you are, happiness is following right behind you.

I left the salon with my hair now perfectly symmetrical and bought groceries for dinner at Safeway. By the time I headed back to my car, the wind had picked up. It felt as if the temperature had dropped twenty degrees. An elderly woman stood near the bus stop. There were tears in her eyes. Her nose was bright pink.

"Excuse me, are you alright?" I asked.

"I've been waiting for the bus to take me home. I don't know when it's coming. I should have checked the schedule before I left my apartment. Do you know where Building 209 is?"

I figured she meant at the Rossmoor Retirement Subdivision, but I'd only been inside the gated community three times so I shook my head. "Do you know how to get there?" I said. "I'm happy to give you a lift home if you direct me."

She smiled. "Would you, dear? It's so cold and I'm not really dressed right."

"Wait here. I'll bring the car around." She shook her head and insisted that she would walk with me. I think she was scared I'd leave without her.

A few minutes later I pulled up to her door. "You're very kind to do this," she said. "Thank you."

"No, thank you. It's been a pleasure chatting with you."

I sat at the table that evening with Austin and Zack and told them all about the people in the salon, how content most of them seemed, and how the experience had made me feel so fortunate. But soon the conversation came around to Austin's most recent complaint: "I'm the only one in my class who doesn't have a cell phone. This kid just got a two hundred dollar phone."

"Too bad Bill Gates won't adopt you," I teased. "Maybe he'd buy you a phone, so God forbid, you wouldn't have to use an old-fashioned house line. For now, though, you'll just have to learn to be content."

He rolled his eyes. "You know how lame you sound?"

I looked at him and his brother and smiled. "Have I ever told you guys about the young rabbit who kept chasing his tail?"